◉ TO MY PARENTS ◉

THE MUSIC OF DJANGO REINHARDT

JAZZ PERSPECTIVES

Lewis Porter, Series General Editor

OTHER BOOKS OF INTEREST

THE MUSIC OF
DJANGO REINHARDT

Benjamin Givan

THE UNIVERSITY OF MICHIGAN PRESS

Ann Arbor

2013   2012   2011   2010   4   3   2   1

A CIP catalog record for this book is available from the British Library.

Library of Congress Cataloging-in-Publication Data

Givan, Benjamin Marx.
    The music of Django Reinhardt / Benjamin Givan.
        p. cm. — (Jazz perspectives)
    Includes bibliographical references (p.   ), discography (p.   ),
    and index.
        ISBN 978-0-472-11499-3 (cloth : alk. paper) —
        ISBN 978-0-472-03408-6 (pbk. : alk. paper)
        1. Reinhardt, Django, 1910-1953—Criticism and interpretation.
    2. Jazz—France—History and criticism.   I. Title.
    ML419.R44G58   2010
    787.87'165092—dc22   2009038400

◉ CONTENTS ◉

Preface *ix*

Acknowledgments *xiii*

⦿ PREFACE ⦿

Recent years have seen an extraordinary flowering of interdisciplinary scholarship on music of all kinds. This positive trend has had very different implications for current research on Western classical music than it has for studies of jazz, which is this book's focus, and all other idioms. For classical music, interdisciplinarity arrived on the heels of a long tradition of musicological and theoretical research focused above all on the music itself (mainly notated scores). This was not so for jazz, which a half century ago had no sooner begun to be regarded as a worthwhile field of inquiry when some writers began to question whether it was even politically appropriate to scrutinize its musical characteristics. LeRoi Jones (Amiri Baraka), for one, argued in 1963 that jazz was fundamentally a sociological phenomenon and only "concomitantly musical."[1]

As a result, some of the important recent research illuminating jazz's social contexts and meanings has rather mystified the music's structural dimension; a recent study of jazz criticism declares that our direct experience of the music itself is "finally elusive."[2] There are, to be sure, good reasons to be wary of close readings; owing to their inherent bias toward European aesthetic values of autonomy and unity, they are not equipped to deal with the full spectrum of jazz's cultural functions and meanings. Yet at the same time I am inclined to agree with the ethnomusicologist Michael Tenzer that "the sharing of [music's] cultural and personal significance has limits without the basis structure provides. We need to hear structure to give our diverse personal interpretations a common orientation."[3] Whether or not modes of analysis that were originally intended for classical music can ever reveal anything worthwhile about other repertoires is another legitimate question, but surely, as the popular music scholar John Covach has reflected, "[T]he time to judge the fruitfulness of an approach is *after* a significant amount of sophisticated work has been done."[4]

The present volume, a music-analytical study of the Belgian-born jazz guitarist Django Reinhardt (1910–53), joins a quite small number of book-length monographs devoted to the musical (rather than the biographical or cultural) legacies of individual jazz artists.[5] Reinhardt's life history, which the introduction will briefly mention, is a fascinating one that has deservedly been the subject of several biographies. This book, however, only substantively addresses biographical details in its first chapter, which investigates how Reinhardt's guitar playing was affected by a severe hand injury he suffered early in his career. The second and third chapters deal with two aspects of his improvisational style. One—his frequent use of discontinuous musical techniques—is an especially distinctive feature of his playing, and the other—his use of a consistent vocabulary of melodic formulas—he shares with virtually all musical improvisers. These chapters' observations are then brought to bear on three complete musical solos from the peak of his career, which are analyzed in depth in chapter 4. The final chapter surveys how Reinhardt's musical language evolved during the last few years of his life as the style he had formed during the swing era of the 1930s began to be influenced by bebop. For the most part, my approach is not overtly evaluative. I hope simply to advance our understanding of several dimensions of the guitarist's playing that have hitherto received little serious attention; readers will naturally draw their own conclusions as to the music's merit. Needless to say, I believe Reinhardt's legacy rewards close analysis and will continue to do so for years to come.

Since jazz has always been a primarily aural expression (Reinhardt did not read music), its musical sounds must be converted into a tangible and permanent form before they can be examined in detail. Accordingly, I rely heavily on Western musical notation transcribed from Reinhardt's recordings. While transcriptions are currently the only practical means of visually representing sonic details in a widely comprehensible way, they are inherently problematic in that they translate performed music into a medium for which it was not intended and for which it is sometimes ill-suited. Therefore, even though I have tried to notate Reinhardt's playing as clearly and accurately as I can, readers are strongly urged to listen to the original recordings if at all possible. The solo guitar lines are notated in treble clef, sounding an octave lower than written (indicated by a number 8 beneath the clef), and lead-sheet-style chord symbols shown above the staff (C7 = C dominant-seventh, and so forth) describe the harmonies played by Reinhardt's accompanying rhythm section on the recordings (as opposed to either the chords implied by his guitar playing alone or, in the case of "standard" popular songs, the chords that appear in published versions; none of these necessarily agree). Measures are generally numbered by both chorus number and measure number within the given chorus (m. 3.5, for example, refers to the fifth bar of the third chorus), and each transcription begins with an indication of how much time has elapsed from the start of the recorded track by that point (1:42, for instance, means that the transcription starts one minute and forty-two seconds into the recording).

◉ ACKNOWLEDGMENTS ◉

Many, many thanks are due to the following people, all of whom provided invaluable support of various kinds—moral, intellectual, technical, editorial, and financial—while I was writing this book: Ramon Satyendra at the University of Michigan; Patrick McCreless, Robert P. Morgan, and John Szwed at Yale University; Chris Hebert, Editor at large for Popular Music and Jazz, and Scott Griffith, Editorial Associate, both at the University of Michigan Press; Series Editor Lewis Porter of Rutgers University, Newark; my colleagues in the Music Department at Skidmore College, especially the department's administrator, Michele Koskinen; Skidmore's Vice President for Academic Affairs, Susan Kress, and Dean of the Faculty, Muriel Poston; Skidmore's Faculty Development Committee; Amy Syrell of the Interlibrary Loan Department at Skidmore's Lucy Scribner Library; Henry Martin, E. Taylor Atkins, Mark Burford, Todd Millstein, Linda Hall, and Alice, Curt, and Becky Givan.

INTRODUCTION

Jazz's origins are hard to pin down. Although the city of New Orleans, home to early-twentieth-century pioneers such as Jelly Roll Morton, Sidney Bechet, and Louis Armstrong, is widely considered its birthplace, the music was a nationwide American phenomenon from almost the very beginning; many of these founders' comparably influential contemporaries were raised far from the mouth of the Mississippi, in places such as New Brunswick, New Jersey (James P. Johnson), Cuthbert, Georgia (Fletcher Henderson), Washington, DC (Duke Ellington), and Davenport, Iowa (Bix Beiderbecke). And curiously enough, in 1910 a musician who ranks among them in the jazz pantheon first saw the light of day in a caravan parked outside the Belgian village of Liberchies, near the French border.

Born to a family of traveling Manouche gypsy entertainers, Jean "Django" Reinhardt lacked formal schooling and remained functionally illiterate well into adulthood.[1] Consequently his biographers, with almost no written primary sources at their disposal, have only been able to draw on the documented reminiscences of his contemporaries and broader contextual historical material.[2] Needless to say, the guitarist left no autograph manuscripts or published scores that might aid a musically oriented study such as the present one. His nine-hundred-plus recordings are the principal surviving sources of reliable information about his music.[3]

Reinhardt's first instrument was the violin; he continued to play it informally in later life, including on two recordings from 1942. At about the age of twelve he took up the banjo-guitar (a six-stringed banjo tuned like a guitar), and was soon performing with small musette ensembles in urban French cafés.[4] In late 1928 his budding professional career was abruptly interrupted when he suffered a devastating hand injury, which is discussed extensively in this book's first chapter. Only during his long recovery from this setback did he finally settle, in his late teens, on the steel-stringed acoustic guitar as his main instrument. Around the same time, he became seriously committed to playing jazz, which was by then France's dominant popular music. Indeed, jazz (and, previously, ragtime) had been a major cultural force in France for almost as long as it had been in the United States.

Even before Reinhardt's birth, France hosted many touring African American musical performers, from classical soloists to minstrel and ragtime ensembles. Of special historical significance was the 1903 production, at Paris's Olympia Theater, of Will Marion Cook's operetta *In Dahomey,* featuring the famous vaudeville duo of George Walker and Bert Williams.[5] Over the next decade increasing numbers of African American musicians began settling in France for extended stays; by World War I many were fixtures on the local entertainment scene, including the drummer Louis Mitchell, whose band began a residency at Le Casino de Paris in 1917. When the United States entered the war that year, thousands of its servicemen arrived on French soil, hastening the influx of American cultural products into the nation's daily life.[6] A key date in jazz's international diffusion was January 1, 1918, when Lt. James Reese Europe's Fifteenth Infantry "Hellfighters" Band, the leading performers of black American "syncopated" music, docked at Brest Harbor. This legendary ensemble toured twenty-five French cities at a time when jazz was still only a nascent presence on the U.S. mainstream scene (less than a year had passed since the Original Dixieland Jazz Band made some of the first recognized jazz recordings).

In the wake of Europe's tour, even more black American artists and entertainers began visiting France, and by the 1920s a vibrant African American expatriate community was thriving in the Parisian district of Montmartre.[7] Among the jazz musicians who arrived in the city during these years were the trumpeters Arthur Briggs and Bill Coleman, both of whom later recorded with Reinhardt, as well as Billy Arnold and his Novelty Jazz Band, white musicians whom the guitarist may have heard in person as a teenager.[8] Most notably, in 1919 Sidney Bechet, the clarinetist and soprano saxophonist who arguably ranked behind only Louis Armstrong among the era's greatest jazz soloists, performed in Paris with Cook's Southern Syncopated Orchestra. The Swiss conductor Ernest Ansermet's review of Bechet's playing is today renowned as one of the earliest instances of an American jazz artist being lauded in print by a prestigious concert musician.[9] Bechet spent a good part of the next decade in the French capital—he appeared alongside Josephine Baker in the *Revue Nègre* of 1925—until being expelled following his incarceration for a firearms violation. In 1950 he settled in France permanently.[10]

French audiences of the 1920s, especially Parisians, clearly heard a lot of African American music in live performance and on records. But since the music was not part of their heritage they were not exposed to it during these early years in as many informal social contexts as were their American counterparts. So it took a while for French musicians to familiarize themselves with jazz. In the immediate postwar years, the best-remembered efforts to this end were made by art music composers; the collective known as Les Six, as well as non-French modernists such as Igor Stravinsky, Paul Hindemith, and Kurt Weill, all wrote works influenced by jazz's rhythmic syncopation, free polyphony, and harmonies, if not, on the whole, its use of improvisation or swing rhythms.[11]

Meanwhile, many French popular musicians strove to play jazz in something closer to its original form. Several became fixtures of Paris's musical life by the late 1920s, among them Ray Ventura, Grégor (Krikor Kelekian, an Armenian immigrant), and André Ekyan (in whose band the violinist Stéphane Grappelli was playing in 1931 when he first met Reinhardt at the Croix du Sud nightclub in Montparnasse). Still, French attitudes toward jazz remained conflicted for quite some time, as the historian Jeffrey Jackson has shown.[12] On the one hand, American musicians were in great public demand because many listeners regarded them as inherently superior to French players, an attitude that often betrayed long-standing primitivist racial stereotypes about African American culture. On the other, many French professional musicians resented being displaced by foreigners. As jazz's popularity grew, some activists responded by promoting local alternatives such as the musette music that Reinhardt played in his youth.[13] Others successfully lobbied for legal quotas that would limit the number of foreign musicians a venue could hire at a time.[14] A more constructive outcome of this nativism was a growing desire to cultivate local jazz players who might compete with Americans at a comparable artistic level.

The institutional center of French pro-jazz activism was the Hot Club of France, founded in 1932 and led for much of its first decade by two of the era's most influential writers on jazz, Hugues Panassié and Charles Delaunay. Although its original mission was to support and popularize specifically African American jazz, a long-standing cause of Panassié's, the Hot Club soon began fostering homegrown talent too. In late 1934 it sponsored the debut performance of the Quintet of the Hot Club of France, the ensemble with which Reinhardt's and Grappelli's names will forever be linked and whose subsequent fame has probably done more to memorialize the Hot Club in history than any of the organization's other ventures. The fact that the Quintet's members were all French (or, strictly speaking, Belgian born in Reinhardt's case) reflected a conception of jazz as an art that had transcended its African American cultural roots, retaining its identity in an entirely new social setting. Even the group's music differed from most American jazz in its all-string instrumentation: a pair of rhythm guitarists plus a string bass accompanying the two soloists. It only really qualified as jazz if the idiom was defined by its formal pitch and rhythmic characteristics. It is probably no coincidence that one of today's most famous advocates of this formalist perspective is the French composer and critic André Hodeir, who first crossed paths with Delaunay in the mid-1930s and recorded in 1943 as a jazz violinist, under the pseudonym Claude Laurence, with Reinhardt's younger brother Joseph (one of the Quintet's founding members). The essence of jazz, as Hodeir sees it, lies in neither its socioeconomic context nor its instrumentation but in a pair of musical features amply exhibited by the Quintet: "swing and hot playing."[15]

Hodeir's narrow structural view of the idiom, based on traditional European notions of aesthetic autonomy that dovetailed conveniently with interwar French musicians' economic self-interest, has fallen out of favor with today's influential culturally oriented school of jazz scholarship. Such present-day scholars often treat the music as more of a sociological phenomenon, defining it as the creative expression of a certain ethnic group—African Americans—subject to specific historical conditions.[16] In the case of a cultural outsider such as Reinhardt, however, musical concerns are pivotal even in determining his individual social context for they are his point of connection with the American jazz world. Only after he had mastered jazz's musical principles—improvisation, swing rhythms, the American popular song repertory, and so forth—was he able not only to play with the Quintet but also to collaborate successfully with major American jazz musicians such as Coleman Hawkins, Benny Carter, and Duke Ellington.

One of Ellington's sidemen, the cornetist Rex Stewart, who recorded with Reinhardt in 1939 and 1947, later paid tribute to the guitarist's artistry, writing, "Django, in my opinion, was to the guitar what Louis

Armstrong was to the trumpet or Art Tatum to the piano. He inspired the playing and thinking of countless hundreds of guitar players all over the world."[17] True to Stewart's pronouncement, Reinhardt was sought out by several leading American guitarists who visited France shortly after World War II, including Charlie Byrd, Les Paul, and Barney Kessel.[18] Other players who subsequently cited him as an influence include the premier hard bop guitarist Wes Montgomery, country musician Chet Atkins, bluesman B. B. King, fusion pioneer John McLaughlin, and even rock-oriented artists Carlos Santana and Vernon Reid.[19] Of all the European jazz musicians active before World War II, only Reinhardt's colleague Grappelli—whose career was much longer, lasting through the mid-1990s—achieved a comparable level of international recognition.

Where Reinhardt's influence is most apparent today, however, is in the so-called gypsy jazz genre, a subidiom cast very much in his image. Some of this genre's best-known exponents, such as Boulou Ferré and Stochelo Rosenberg, hail from Western European gypsy communities, but the style has adherents worldwide, droves of whom converge each summer on the French village of Samois-sur-Seine, Reinhardt's final home, for a festival named in his memory. Many, though not all, gypsy jazz musicians focus on re-creating Reinhardt's music of the 1930s, favoring an all-string lineup, a repertoire similar to the Quintet's, and occasionally even fetishizing the guitarist's personal idiosyncrasies and sartorial preferences.[20] At times fidelity to the past takes precedence over individual creativity; even Biréli Lagrène, perhaps the idiom's leading figure and a brilliant musician of considerable stylistic range, often, when playing gypsy jazz, closely replicates Reinhardt's musical language and repertoire.[21]

Paradoxically, gypsy jazz's aesthetic goals are in key respects quite the opposite of Reinhardt's since the style sustains its distinct identity by maintaining those features—above all its instrumentation—that most differentiated the guitarist's music from American jazz. For Reinhardt himself these same features were simply a native musical heritage that he apparently felt no inclination to preserve as he emulated American players. Indeed, as detailed in this book's final chapter, he eventually abandoned many of them in favor of a bebop-influenced style, electric guitar, and standard jazz rhythm section of piano, bass, and drums. As his near contemporary and fellow guitarist Jean "Matelot" Ferret insisted several years after Reinhardt died, "Django did *not* play in the gypsy style. He played a style that was his alone, that began with him.

Certainly, he played the guitar, a traditional [gypsy] instrument, but his school of guitar playing was his own creation."[22] Recently, some writers have begun to construct a retrospective history of gypsy jazz with Reinhardt as its founding figurehead.[23] It is important to remember, though, that this narrative is in many ways an "invented tradition."[24] Reinhardt himself had no conception of "gypsy jazz," and even if he had lived to witness it, he would likely have had little interest in it; his musical idols were Americans such as Armstrong and Ellington, and, later on, Charlie Parker and Dizzy Gillespie.

As a music-analytic study, the present volume is not directly concerned with Reinhardt's unique cultural location at the nexus of Manouche society, the French mainstream, and the American jazz world. Nonetheless, it has some general implications for how we understand the guitarist's social context. By highlighting what Reinhardt shares with American jazz musicians artistically, namely, his music itself, rather than how he differs from them culturally, the following pages implicitly reframe the prevalent American-centered view of the guitarist as an outsider engaged in an African American art form. Granted, Reinhardt was a cultural outsider to the world of jazz, yet the tendency of many writers to cast him as an exotic gypsy Other obscures the fact that he is, if anything, even more anomalous within his native milieu.[25] He has become, for example, a notable exception to the distinctive Manouche ritual of erasing concrete signs of the dead by destroying their belongings and refraining from mentioning their names or commemorating them publicly.[26] Contrary to custom, the Manouche still actively celebrate Reinhardt's name and artistic legacy decades after his passing.[27] By placing his music at center stage, this book highlights the extraordinary individual creativity that sets Reinhardt apart from his gypsy heritage and for which he is venerated as one of the great jazz improvisers of his time.

◉ 1 ◉

LEFT-HAND TECHNIQUE

Over the years, a considerable mystique has surrounded not only Reinhardt's musical legacy but also his singular personal history, which was marked by an early life-altering event. On the night of October 26, 1928, the eighteen-year-old musician returned from a playing engagement to his caravan at a gypsy encampment outside Paris.[1] As he prepared to retire to bed, a candle's open flame accidentally ignited a large pile of celluloid flowers that Bella, his first wife, planned to sell the next day. Bella escaped from the blaze with minor injuries, but the right side of Reinhardt's body was burned so severely that a surgeon at the Hôpital Lariboisière recommended his leg be amputated to prevent gangrene. Reinhardt refused, instead undergoing surgery (under chloroform anesthetic) to open and drain his wounds, which involved the application of silver nitrate to dry the flesh and cause scars to form. During a recovery period of almost two years he regained the use of his leg, but the third and fourth fingers of his left hand were permanently damaged. That Reinhardt managed to relearn his instrument with an entirely new playing technique has been a source of awe and mystery ever since.

Little else is known about Reinhardt's accident or, for that matter, his early life in general. The musette music that he began playing in his early teens was an urban vernacular form that emerged during the late nineteenth century and remained popular as live entertainment in France in the years after World War I. It bears little musical resemblance to jazz. Indeed, the art historian Jody Blake notes that even though musette orchestras—typically three- or four-piece accordion-led ensembles—might superficially seem like a sort of "French equivalent of the jazz band," the *bals-musettes* (working-class dance halls) where the music was often played were viewed by contemporary artists such as Jean Cocteau and his circle as the site of an authentically Gallic culture free of the American influences that pervaded postwar French life.[2] Reinhardt's conversion from musette to jazz soon after his accident may not have been the only reason he concurrently exchanged his banjo-guitar for a standard guitar. The historian Alain Antonietto raises the possibility that Reinhardt made the change during his convalescence because the guitar required a lighter touch on the fingerboard and thus was less physically demanding.[3] The biographer François Billard adds that, in contrast to the banjo's piercing sonority, the guitar's mellower sound may have been better suited to the hospital ward where Reinhardt spent his recovery since it would have been less disruptive to the other patients.[4]

The jazz recordings that Reinhardt heard while recovering from his injury probably included those of Eddie Lang (1902–33), the American jazz guitarist whose partnership with the violinist Joe Venuti during the late 1920s and early 1930s is the clearest historical precedent for the Quintet of the Hot Club of France's all-string instrumentation.[5] The extent of Lang's influence on Reinhardt is uncertain. Stéphane Grappelli later remembered that soon after he and Reinhardt met in the early 1930s "we decided every day to do like Eddie Lang and Joe Venuti to amuse ourselves,"[6] but Reinhardt was also said to have later spoken dismissively of Lang's playing.[7] Still, the American's records would have at least made him aware of the guitar's possibilities in jazz at the very time that he was adopting both a new instrument and a new musical idiom.

In the absence of concrete information, many writers have tended to romanticize Reinhardt's biography, often exaggerating his disability either because of misconceptions or for rhetorical effect. Tales of the enigmatic gypsy who miraculously triumphed over dire personal circumstances make for compelling reading but not necessarily for historical accuracy. This chapter seeks to answer two straightforward questions: what was the nature of Reinhardt's injury and how did it affect his music? The best sources of evidence are films, photographs, and above all sound recordings. Transcriptions are especially useful for comparing his playing before and after the accident and for contrasting his instrumental technique with that of an able-bodied performer (in this case Eddie Lang). Before addressing these, it is worth briefly considering the physiological implications of Reinhardt's injury from a clinical perspective.

At the very least, photographs show that the third and fourth fingers of Reinhardt's left hand were, as Ian Cruickshank writes, "deformed" or, in Mike Peters's words, "partially mangled."[8] But many writers disagree as to whether the affected fingers remained functional. Mike Zwerin, like several other authors, writes that the fingers were paralyzed, although he adds that the guitarist was still able to use these fingers to an extent.[9] To the contrary, Michael James, in an article in *The New Grove Dictionary of Jazz,* states unequivocally that Reinhardt's accident "deprived him of the use of two fingers."[10] Likewise, biographer Patrick Williams claims that the guitarist's handicap "allowed him only to play notes with three fingers of his hand: the middle finger, the index finger, and the thumb."[11] In fact, there is much evidence that Reinhardt actually retained a significant, if substantially limited, level of function in his damaged fingers. A valuable source of reference when interpreting this evidence is the medical literature on hand burns.

The anatomy of the human hand is extraordinarily complex. Its skeletal structure consists of nineteen bones and seventeen joints. Each finger contains three bones, called phalanges (the thumb has only two), and the joint between two phalanges is called an interphalangeal joint. At the base of each finger the longest phalange meets another bone, a metacarpal, at the metacarpophalangeal joint. The metacarpals are in turn attached to the carpals, a group of small bones within the wrist. Motion is controlled by two sets of muscles attached to the bones with tendons. Extrinsic muscles, located in the forearm, are responsible for powerful motion, while intrinsic muscles, located within the hand itself, control delicate, finely coordinated movements.[12] A total of thirty-nine muscles control hand and wrist motion, and there is considerable interdependence: moving one part of the hand often affects the position of another. Finger movement is described as either flexion, when joints are bent toward the palm, or extension, when joints are bent away from the palm.[13]

When the hand is burned by flames, as was Reinhardt's, the damage is most often to the back (dorsum) of the hand ("probably because the back of the hand is exposed when it is used to protect the face and because the hand closes instinctively in flash burns").[14] Burns are classified according to their severity as either "partial thickness," when they are fairly superficial and produce blistering and minor scarring, or "full thickness," when the skin's entire thickness is charred, leaving an open wound that heals with scar tissue lacking the skin's former elasticity.[15] Additionally, "deep burns of the dorsum of the hand are apt to destroy the extensor tendons, especially those over the middle joints of the fingers," which inhibits extension of the affected digits.[16] Severe burns to the dorsum of the hand frequently lead to hyperextension of the metacarpophalangeal joints and compensatory flexion of the interphalangeal joints.[17] That is, the fingers are drawn backward at their base joint while their smaller joints curl inward. Photographs show that the permanent effects of Reinhardt's injury almost exactly corresponded to these conditions: the third and fourth fingers of his left hand were bent backward at their base at an abnormal angle, and the upper joints were partially flexed.[18]

Recent decades have seen great advances in all fields of medicine, the treatment of hand injuries being no exception. Doctors are now often able to prevent deformities by using splints to support and protect the burned hand during recovery. In 1928, however, Reinhardt benefited only from care designed to stave off potentially life-threatening infections and otherwise had to cope with his injuries without further treatment. Although his left hand clearly was disfigured, the view of some authors that two of his digits were "useless" or "paralyzed" is misleading. Indeed, the relevant medical literature is notable for the conspicuous absence of the word *paralysis*. Providing that muscle tissue and tendons heal sufficiently, a burned hand may retain a significant level of function within the constrictions of its deformed state.

Several commentators have rightly acknowledged that Reinhardt could still use his damaged fingers. A short discographical booklet published in 1944 by Billy Neill and E. Gates states that:

> [Reinhardt] uses the first and second left-hand fingers most of the time in single-note work; in chord work he can make use of the third and fourth fingers to a limited extent on the first two strings. He plays his famous octave passages on any two strings, with a "damped" string in between. . . , avoiding that frenzied rushing up and down the fingerboard which would otherwise be necessary. His famous chromatic runs, if played in the first position, are *fingered;* if played up the fingerboard, they are *glissed* with one finger. He plays unusual chord shapes because of his handicap.[19]

This may be an eyewitness description, although, since Reinhardt spent World War II in continental Europe and the booklet was published in England, the authors would probably not, in 1944, have seen him in person for at least five years. It is supported by a definite firsthand account from Reinhardt's longtime colleague Grappelli, who recalled shortly after the guitarist's death that "he acquired amazing dexterity with those first two fingers, but that didn't mean he never employed the others. He learned to grip the guitar with his little finger on the E string and the next finger on the B. That accounts for some of those chord progressions which Django was probably the first to perform on the guitar . . . at least in the jazz idiom."[20]

Some recent writers, such as Mike Peters, have repeated Grappelli's claim that Reinhardt was able to use his disabled fingers on the guitar's two highest strings but that these fingers were only used to play chords, while single-string melodies were played with just the two fully functional digits.[21] Peters also notes that Reinhardt's hands appear to have been larger than average. The critic Whitney Balliett, like Grappelli, speculates that Reinhardt's physical condition may have been partially responsible for his innovative harmonic techniques: "The huge hand made the crippled fingers work nonetheless: thus the mysterious chords and melodic lines that no one had heard before."[22]

But these accounts amount to little more than brief asides. A far more detailed and rigorous consideration of Reinhardt's instrumental technique appears in Alexander Schmitz and Peter Maier's biography.[23] Schmitz and Maier begin by asserting that for chord playing "the third finger of Django's left hand was almost always completely functional, so long as it was not required to stretch far from the middle finger."[24] They agree that Reinhardt's use of his damaged fingers was primarily confined to the instrument's two highest-pitched strings (the B and high E), which prohibited him from playing those chords that demand considerable wrist supination in order to place the third or fourth fingers on the instrument's middle or lower strings.[25] This precludes many fingerings that are merely run-of-the-mill for nondisabled guitarists. The authors also suggest that Reinhardt was able to take advantage of his disability in various ways, for example by barring across up to three strings with his third finger, which fell naturally at an angle more conducive to this technique than it would on a healthy hand.[26] They do not, however, support their findings with specific evidence of the guitarist's technique in practice, of which there is of course plenty.

In the late 1990s a short film featuring Reinhardt and the Quintet was discovered.[27] *Le Jazz Hot,* made while the group toured England in 1938, begins with a brief staged "Introduction to Jazz," demonstrated by a studio orchestra with an explanatory voice-over. Reinhardt then appears playing the theme "Tornerai (J'Attendrai)," first alone, next joined by Grappelli in a duet, and finally with the Quintet's rhythm section. Although the guitarist is on camera for only a few brief stretches, he plainly uses only his index and middle fingers on the fretboard while soloing melodically, corroborating the descriptions of his single-note technique cited earlier. His unaccompanied introduction also includes some chordal playing, and he unmistakably uses his disabled third and fourth fingers at several points. A number of still photographs of Reinhardt playing also confirm that he was able to use both his third and fourth fingers on the guitar's uppermost strings to play chords.[28] Yet photographs present only static records of a dynamic physical activity; for more clues, recordings provide much additional information.

To gauge the impact of Reinhardt's injury on his guitar technique, we can begin by comparing his playing before the October 1928 accident with that of his later career. He made fifteen known recordings between May and October of 1928. On each he has a solely accompanimental role as banjo-guitarist within a three-part musette ensemble dominated by an accordionist and also featuring at various times a whistler, slide-whistle, xylophone, or other percussion. The recordings are less than ideal historical sources because their sound quality is poor and even the original pitch is uncertain. (The original instrumental tunings are not known for sure, and, as is not infrequently the case with recordings of this vintage, inconsistent turntable speeds at any stage of the recording and reproduction process may have distorted the sounding pitch.)[29] Furthermore, because Reinhardt is featured only as an accompanist, his playing is sometimes difficult to hear beneath the lead instruments. For these reasons, the transcription process involves a certain amount of guesswork.

Example 1.1 transcribes a short passage from "Miss Columbia" (9–10/28; mx. H 966-B), a tune that Reinhardt (identified on the original record label as "Jeangot") recorded with the accordionist Marceau Verschueren in the fall of 1928, just weeks before the caravan fire.[30] The transcription gives a hypothetical tablature for Reinhardt's banjo-guitar accompaniment, following standard notational conventions and assuming that, as most sources suggest, the banjo-guitar's strings are tuned identically to standard guitar tuning (E2–A2–D3–G3–B3–E4).[31] Accordingly, the six tablature lines represent the instrument's six strings, with the lowest pitched (E2) represented by the lowest line. Directly beneath each note (or chord) on the ordinary treble-clef staff, the tablature indicates which string is sounded and at which fret number. For instance, a zero appearing on the highest line of the tablature staff indicates that the guitar's high E string is sounded as an open string; likewise, the number 2 written on the next-to-highest line indicates that the B string is sounded while being depressed at the second fret (producing the pitch C♯4, two half steps higher).

0:03

EXAMPLE 1.1. Performance of "Miss Columbia" (9–10/28; mx. H 966-B)

Unsurprisingly, having at the time a fully functional left hand, Reinhardt uses all four fingers on "Miss Columbia." In the given excerpt he plays an "oompah" accompaniment: in four-four time, a bass line played on the instrument's middle and lower strings on beats one and three alternates with chords played on the higher strings on beats two and four. The descending half-note bass progression E–D♯–C♯–B is probably played using the left pinkie and middle finger on the pitches C♯ and B respectively. These two notes are played on the instrument's A string at the fourth and second fret while the first finger depresses the G string at the first fret. Thus, the wrist is heavily supinated, enabling the fourth finger to reach across the fingerboard. Such a fingering, while quotidian in the hands of any modestly accomplished guitarist, would have been entirely impossible for Reinhardt after 1928.

Yet he was still playing the same sorts of accompaniments a decade later and in a jazz style that was more harmonically and texturally varied. Example 1.2 transcribes the beginning of a 1938 recording of "It Had To Be You" in which Reinhardt alone accompanied Grappelli's violin (2/1/38; mx. DTB 3533-1) (his solo guitar introduction is omitted). A proposed tablature and left-hand fingering for the guitar part are also given. The left-hand fingering is displayed between the guitar staff and tablature with the index finger through the pinkie numbered 1–4 and the thumb labeled "T." Where Reinhardt strikes two or more notes simultaneously, the fingering numbers are arranged vertically, with the highest-sounding string (usually also the highest-sounding pitch) at the top and the others in order beneath it. The first chord in m. 1.1, for instance, is played with the middle finger (2) placed across both the A and D strings at the fifth fret (sounding the pitches D3 and G3), the index finger (1) on the G string at the fourth fret (sounding the pitch B3), and the ring finger (3) on the B string at the fifth fret (sounding E4).

The given tablature and fingering suggest that instead of using his weaker fingers to play a bass line within an oompah accompaniment, as he did in 1928, Reinhardt would often play the bass line with his first and second fingers and create chords by barring across the higher strings with any of his first three fingers. The chords in mm. 1.3–1.4, 1.9–1.10, and 1.15–1.16, for example, all have the third finger barred across the upper three strings. Alternatively, Reinhardt could use his thumb for the bass line by curling it over the guitar neck so as to reach the instrument's lowest two strings (as in mm. 1.2 and 1.11–1.13). While able-bodied guitarists also sometimes find it convenient to use the left thumb in this way,[32] Reinhardt probably had to rely on it more because he had fewer alternatives. The three- and four-note chords in "It Had To Be You" illustrate that, in addition to using harmonies requiring only his healthy index and middle fingers, Reinhardt frequently employed his disabled third finger too. None of the chords in example 1.2 calls for the fourth finger on the left hand (although since the indicated fingerings are merely speculative it is conceivable that he used it).

More of Reinhardt's chord-playing techniques are displayed in the unaccompanied performance transcribed in example 1.3, an excerpt from a 1937 recording of "A Little Love, A Little Kiss" (4/26/37; mx. OLA 1716-1). The passage shown is from an a cappella rendition of the song's verse that follows a short violin and guitar introduction and precedes the rhythm section's entry for the solo choruses (again, a proposed tablature and left-hand fingering are given).[33] None of the thirty-seven chords shown in this example requires the guitarist's fourth finger (some of the chords are repeated, so there are only about twenty-five or so different chords). Fifteen do, however, use the third finger; in each instance Reinhardt uses it only to depress the instrument's high E string, with the possible exception of the final chord in m. 5. This particular chord (G–C♯–E♯–A) may have been played with the third finger on the B string, as indicated, although it is also playable by using the second finger to depress simultaneously both the G and B strings.

But if Reinhardt did indeed play the music in example 1.3 without using his left pinkie, he would in several instances have had to stretch

EXAMPLE 1.2. Improvisation on "It Had To Be You" (2/1/38; mx. DTB 3533-1)

1.8

1.11

1.14

EXAMPLE 1.2. *(cont.)*

EXAMPLE 1.3. Improvisation on "A Little Love, A Little Kiss" (4/26/37; mx. OLA 1716-1)

his ring finger quite far from his middle finger. The first chord in m. 1 (G♯–D–E♯–C♯), the first chord in m. 2 (E–A♯–C♯–A), and the final chord in m. 4 (G♯–D–F♯–C♯) would all require his index finger at a given fret, the second finger a fret higher, and the third finger two more frets higher than the second finger. This appears to contradict Schmitz and Maier's view that Reinhardt was unable to stretch his disabled third finger far from the second (although the guitarist's large hands may not have found this such a stretch). Alternatively, he might have played the highest notes of these chords with his pinkie on the high E string. Without visual evidence, recordings cannot always reveal conclusively how Reinhardt fingered a given chord.

It is possible, though, to generalize about the relationship between the guitarist's physical state and his music by comparing his technique with that of an unimpaired performer. Reinhardt's performance of "A Little Love, A Little Kiss" was likely inspired by Eddie Lang's 1927 recording of the same tune (5/28/27; mx. W 80941-D). Lang's version is entirely unaccompanied (Reinhardt is supported by the full Quintet during the rest of his solo, which is not transcribed here). Like Reinhardt, Lang plays the song in D major and begins with a similarly free, rubato rendition of its verse, which is transcribed in example 1.4.[34] Despite their other dissimilarities, these two interpretations of the same theme, one seldom heard in jazz, represent one of the most likely signs of the American's direct influence on Reinhardt.

From a technical standpoint, Lang's version serves as a stark reminder that Reinhardt's disability was, despite his adaptability, considerable. A majority of Lang's chords containing four or more notes would have been unplayable for Reinhardt. Musically speaking, Lang therefore plays many more chords containing intervals of less than a major third between adjacent notes. Since a guitar's strings are tuned in perfect fourths, except for the major third between the G and B strings, a player wishing to create intervals smaller than the interval between any two adjacent open strings must heavily supinate his or her wrist so as to stop a given string at a higher fret than that of the neighboring higher string. For instance, in m. 7 of example 1.4, Lang creates a major second, G–A, by stopping the B string at the eighth fret with his pinkie and the high E string at the fifth fret with his index finger. This requires wrist supination so that the fourth finger can reach a lower string than the first finger. Lang employs various other chord fingerings with similar physical demands; they are indicated in example 1.4 wherever a left-hand finger number appears beneath a lower finger number, such as in

EXAMPLE 1.4. Improvisation on "A Little Love, A Little Kiss" (5/28/27; mx. W 80941-D), performed by Eddie Lang

EXAMPLE 1.4. *(cont.)*

m. 1, where the fourth finger depresses the G string while the second finger stops the B string. Even though Reinhardt could use these sorts of fingerings, too, with his healthy index and middle fingers, he tended to heavily favor chords in which any two adjacent strings are stopped at the same fret (e.g., by barring with a single finger) or in which a given string is stopped at a higher fret than its lower neighbor. This is especially the case with the interval between the highest pair of notes in Reinhardt's chosen chords, which are most often played on the instrument's uppermost strings (tuned at the interval of a perfect fourth). In other words, Reinhardt's chords usually contain an interval of at least a perfect fourth between their highest two pitches. Lang, of course, often used such formations as well (they are, after all, also easier for a nondisabled person to play). But overall he used many more closely voiced harmonies than Reinhardt did.

The foregoing evidence confirms that, although Reinhardt's injury greatly constrained his instrumental technique, he retained a substantial degree of function in the disfigured third finger of his left hand. And though his disability greatly limited the range of chords available to him, ruling out many close voicings, he was partially able to compensate for it, for instance by using his thumb to play bass notes on the guitar's lower strings. Still, his use of the thumb and disabled fingers seems to have been associated solely with chord playing. All evidence suggests that when soloing with single-string melodies he relied on only his fully functional index and middle fingers.

Because Reinhardt's recordings from before the accident feature him only as an accompanist, they present very few examples of single-string playing for comparison with his later work. But on several brief occasions the young musician used arpeggiated harmonies or a counter-melody instead of his customary chordal accompaniment. Example 1.5 transcribes one such instance from "Moi Aussi" (9–10/28; mx. 968-A), recorded at the same 1928 session as "Miss Columbia." Here, while accordionist Verschueren and a whistler (identified on the original label as simply "Erardy") state the melody in unison, Reinhardt plays an obbligato-like melodic accompaniment based on rising and falling two-octave arpeggiations of a dominant-seventh harmony (B7 in the key of E major). The proposed fingering given beneath the guitar staff suggests that he may have used all four left-hand fingers, traversing all of the instrument's strings but the lowest. This would have allowed his hand to remain between the fingerboard's sixth and tenth frets rather than shifting up and down the guitar neck. In the wake of his injury such fingerings were often no longer feasible.

For comparison, some examples of Reinhardt's mature single-string solo work appear in example 1.6, which shows excerpts from a performance of "Sweet Georgia Brown" (12/21/37; mx. OLA 2220-1) that he recorded in 1937 as a duet with Grappelli accompanying at the piano. In example 1.6a the guitarist plays a diminished-seventh arpeggiation that ascends almost two octaves from F♯3 through D♯5 (as will be seen in

EXAMPLE 1.5. Performance of "Moi Aussi" (9–10/28; mx. 968-A)

chapter 3, this is one of his favored melodic formulas). When fingered using only the index and middle fingers, this figure is most comfortably executed by progressively shifting the left hand from the instrument's fourth fret up to the eleventh (and finally the twelfth). A guitarist with all fingers available could, using a more orthodox fingering such as that shown in example 1.6b, execute the same figure while remaining between the seventh and twelfth frets.[35]

Examples 1.6c and 1.6d, from the same solo, are both melodic sequences incorporating a repeated open string. Example 1.6c, another of Reinhardt's melodic formulas, is an ascending sequence in which the guitar's open D string provides a pedal tone beneath a series of triplet arpeggiations. It can be played using only the first two fingers of the left hand in alternation across adjacent strings (which requires considerable physical coordination to accomplish at Reinhardt's tempo of quarter note = 204). In example 1.6d the guitarist plays a chromatically descending sequence of triplets consisting of broken octaves, struck with two downstrokes in his right hand, interspersed with upstrokes sounding the open E string. He plays the broken octaves with his left forefinger depressing the G string and another finger—perhaps the middle finger, as notated here, but quite possibly one of the disabled fingers—on the high E string. Simultaneous octave doublings were one of Reinhardt's trademark techniques; example 1.6e shows an instance from the solo's closing measures. As described earlier by Neill and Gates, the octaves are sounded by depressing two nonadjacent strings while a single intervening string is damped by light pressure from the first finger.

The astonishing facility with which Reinhardt executed these sorts of rapid, technically daunting effects was a milestone in the historical evolution of guitar technique. Despite his handicap, Reinhardt can yet be regarded as a forerunner of the cult of guitar virtuosity that has emerged in recent decades. Neither his predecessors, such as Eddie Lang, nor other swing era guitarists, such as Charlie Christian (1916–42), equaled Reinhardt's technical achievements in terms of sheer physical speed. But since World War II, and particularly with the rise of the electric guitar, guitarists of all stripes have often placed a premium on velocity. (Within the gypsy jazz genre that Reinhardt inspired, this tendency has sometimes been criticized for prioritizing physical technique over artistic substance.)[36] Although such a broad trend cannot be credited to any single individual, Reinhardt set an important precedent.

Eventually it was Christian, not Reinhardt, who became the defining influence on future generations of jazz guitarists. Christian's style,

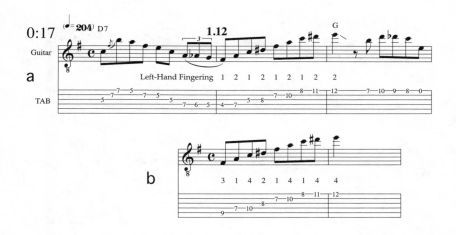

EXAMPLE 1.6. Improvisation on "Sweet Georgia Brown" (12/21/37; mx. OLA 2220-1)

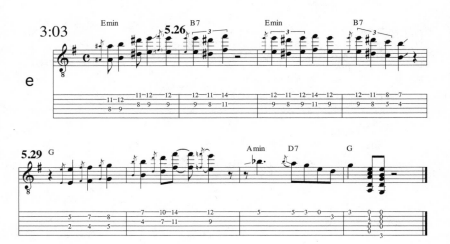

EXAMPLE 1.6. *(cont.)*

shaped principally by the blues and western swing of his Oklahoma origins, as well as the playing of tenor saxophonist Lester Young,[37] showed
few obvious signs of his European contemporary's influence, although
there are intriguing accounts of him replicating Reinhardt's solos from
memory in live concerts.[38] In fact, although the Quintet of the Hot Club
of France's records were available in the United States during the 1930s,
Reinhardt's stateside reputation was still quite modest when Christian
began performing.[39] Later some of Reinhardt's original instrumental
techniques were adopted by other players; octave doublings, for example, reappeared as a signature device in the playing of Wes Montgomery,
the leading jazz guitarist of the 1960s.[40]

The most influential aspect of Reinhardt's guitar playing—his phe-
nomenal digital velocity—was thus, paradoxically, in an area where his
injury might appear to have been most disadvantageous. Misconceptions about his disability have fostered an enduring conundrum: the
handicap seems enormously significant in theory yet spectacularly irrel-
evant in practice. Even if it was less severe than many writers have sug-
gested, Reinhardt's injury nonetheless represented a colossal challenge,
imposing considerable limitations on his instrumental technique. That
he surmounted this challenge attests not so much to the inconsequence
of his affliction as to his extraordinary feat in transcending it.

◉ 2 ◉
MUSICAL DISCONTINUITY

Most analytical literature on jazz has placed a premium on structural unity. Early writers, such as André Hodeir and Gunther Schuller, initially sought to legitimize the music in the musicological community's eyes by demonstrating its accessibility to traditional formalist perspectives.[1] This tendency persists in much current jazz analysis; leading contemporary theorists such as Henry Martin and Steve Larson occasionally give their interpretations an explicitly evaluative slant.[2] Formalists' inclination to view jazz improvisations as autonomous artifacts whose aesthetic value stems from their internal coherence has in recent years been challenged on the grounds that, despite its putative objectivity, it remains as inseparably tied to an inapposite European ideological heritage as the conservatism it opposes. Ethnomusicologists and other culturally oriented scholars have instead preferred to focus on jazz's immediate social context—primarily black American vernacular culture—and its historic roots in sub-Saharan Africa.[3]

A compromise can be found between these opposing standpoints by regarding musical structure and social context as inextricably interdependent.[4] But a further possibility, yet to be seriously considered, is that we might analyze jazz closely without necessarily seeking to identify long-range unifying features. Reinhardt's improvisations provide a fitting case study because they often exhibit striking discontinuities. Even though it is quite possible to analyze his music by showing that coherent designs sometimes underlie its surface-level contrasts (see example 5.1, for instance), the discontinuities are so prominent and pervasive that they call for another approach, one that takes them at face value rather than trying to resolve them.

The critic Whitney Balliett once described Reinhardt's characteristic modus operandi as follows.

> Reinhardt might start a medium-tempo ballad with three or four bars of slightly altered melody, played in single notes behind the beat, each phrase graced by his vibrato (almost a tremble), pause for a beat, and go into a brief mock double-time, rest again, drop in an abrupt, massive chord, and release a hissing upward run. Then he'd cut his volume in half and turn into the bridge with a delicate, fernlike single-note variation of the melody, letting his notes linger and bend and float on his vibrato. Just before the end of the bridge, he would loose another offbeat chord, let it shimmer for three or four beats, work through a humplike arpeggio, lower his volume again, and return to a single-note variation of the original melody and come to rest.[5]

Much of the guitarist's music has this capricious quality; Balliett's description is especially reminiscent of performances such as a 1937 improvisation on "Solitude" (4/21/37; mx. OLA 1706–1) (see example 3.3). In any given solo, Reinhardt might pursue a wide variety of strategies without adhering to any single consistent approach or overarching unifying scheme. Some recurrent techniques recur throughout his oeuvre, though. In examining them, a useful starting point is one of the first written analyses of his playing, published by André Hodeir in 1954.

Hodeir's book *Toward Jazz* briefly discusses Reinhardt's solo on "Solid Old Man" (4/5/39; mx. OSW 67-1), a twelve-bar blues that the guitarist recorded at an April 1939 session with cornetist Rex Stewart, bassist Billy Taylor, and clarinetist Barney Bigard (on this occasion doubling on drums), who were passing through Paris on tour with the Duke Ellington Orchestra. On "Solid Old Man," Reinhardt plays an eight-bar introduction before the opening head and a single solo chorus; the latter is transcribed in example 2.1. Hodeir concludes his analysis with the following insight.

> [T]he curious construction of this blues involves three phrases, divided as follows: [measures] 1–3, 4–7, 10–12. What happens between the first beat of the seventh measure and the first beat of the tenth? Does Django stop playing? Not at all; these three measures contain a fairly long phrase, which *does not belong to the solo proper.* It is part of an orchestral "accompaniment" which

Django "heard in his head" while playing his improvisation. The "parenthetical" character of this phrase should be apparent to every attentive listener.[6]

The phrase Reinhardt plays from m. 7–9 is differentiated from the immediately preceding and following material because of its lower register and distinct motivic profile (a repeated four-note scale segment oscillating between F and B♭). This sort of parenthetical interpolation is typical of the guitarist's music and is therefore worth exploring at some length.

EXAMPLE 2.1. Improvisation on "Solid Old Man" (4/5/39; mx. OSW 67-1)

To begin, consider Hodeir's view that the parenthetical phrase in Reinhardt's solo sounds like an *accompaniment,* subordinate to the surrounding musical material, and that it expresses a musical image that the guitarist *heard in his head.* The latter claim resonates with the testimony of many musicians. Jazz players often describe their improvisations as expressing musical ideas that are first imagined internally; in some cases they claim consciously to "think ahead," usually by no more than a bar or two.[7] Reinhardt's friend and biographer Charles Delaunay told Balliett that the guitarist "had a constant vision of music—a circle of music—in his head. I think he could see his music."[8]

But an improviser's mind is not exclusively occupied with musical thoughts that are realized as sound. In most mainstream jazz styles, performers are guided by a preexistent theme that, by prescribing a fixed temporal-harmonic structure (and in many instances a melody, too), dictates a set of creative constraints that they must also keep in mind. Many say that they retain an inner image of the chord changes while playing, and some use the melody itself as a continual object of reference.[9] One of this chapter's basic premises is that discontinuities within a given improvised solo may result from a performer's attentive shifts between different conceptual fields. This premise also underlies a well-known distinction that Hodeir himself makes in his book *Jazz: Its Evolution and Essence* between "paraphrase improvisation," which is explicitly based on a preexisting melody, and "chorus phrase improvisation," which observes only an established harmonic structure.[10] As Lawrence Gushee has noted, one of Hodeir's basic assumptions is that the improvisational process is based on "separable levels of mental activity."[11] Whereas other authors have both refined and questioned Hodeir's dichotomy, I do not directly adopt or adapt his scheme.[12] Instead, I proceed from the same supposition that different regions of a musical improvisation may have separate conceptual origins, but I ultimately derive some additional hypotheses that are specifically oriented toward Reinhardt's music.

Abrupt discontinuities are found in many musical idioms, often involving effects such as antiphony, ornamental interpolation, and the illusion of simultaneous progression.[13] Such effects are most easily produced by two or more different instruments or groups of instruments. A well-known example of antiphony in classical music is the *cori spezzati* of Renaissance Venice in which separate choirs are positioned apart from one another. In Afro-diasporic culture, antiphony, better known as "call-and-response," originated historically in West African vocal traditions and persists, for instance, in the interplay between pastor and congregation in the black American church; in swing era big-band arrangements when different instrumental sections, or a section and a single soloist, alternate phrases; and in the jazz convention of soloists trading four- or eight-bar statements. Reinhardt uses the latter two techniques on his 1937 recording of "Mabel" (12/14/37; mx. OLA 1997-2), exchanging phrases with both Grappelli's violin and an orchestrated big-band brass section.

Ornamental interpolation, by contrast, typically involves one instrument, or group of instruments, decorating or otherwise complementing a melody played by another. Some writers consider this technique a hallmark of African American music in general, exemplified by the dialogic interaction of voice and guitar in the traditional rural blues.[14] Reinhardt provides a straightforward illustration on his recording of "Studio 24" (4/16/42; mx. 16192), improvising short interjections between each phrase of the theme, which is played by pianist Ivon de Bie. The third noted sort of discontinuity—the illusion of simultaneous progression—is famously exemplified by Igor Stravinsky's *Symphonies of Winds*. In a well-known analysis, Edward T. Cone contends that this work creates its illusion through the "stratification" and "interlock" of distinct juxtaposed strands of musical material; he writes that "each line continues to exert its influence even when silent."[15]

While all these kinds of discontinuity involve at least two different musical instruments or voices, usually played by different performers, the effect that Hodeir identifies in Reinhardt's solo on "Solid Old Man" is conveyed by just a single musician playing one instrument. This, too, is an established practice, especially in jazz. Schuller has compared the jazz pianist Earl Hines's use of dynamics and musical texture, which "distinguish between primary and secondary material," to the interpolative effects found in the nineteenth-century piano works of Chopin and Liszt.[16] Likewise, Paul Berliner notes that jazz horn players sometimes give the impression of improvising both call and response figures on their own; he quotes trumpeter Lonnie Hillyer's explanation that "[O]ne approach [to improvisation] is for me to think of myself as being two players. See, the upper player was one guy and the lower player was another guy. I was telling the story as if there was a dialogue going on between the two players. I've heard Trane and Bird and other players do that kind of thing on records, like they were accompanying themselves."[17] Louis Armstrong used this sort of self-accompaniment in his vocals, which often feature interpolated scatted figures between each line of a song.[18] Even the third category of musical discontinuity, the illusion of simultaneous progression, can be created by a single performer. Charles Hartman has compared certain of Bobby McFerrin's a cappella vocal improvisations (as heard on his 1984 solo album *The Voice*) to the *style brisé* of J. S. Bach's works for unaccompanied violin and cello; both use registral contrast to create the impression of simultaneously unfolding contrapuntal lines (somewhat analogous to Cone's interpretation of Stravinsky, though on a more condensed time scale).[19]

Cone and others have written extensively about discontinuity in Western art music, but their work currently has no parallel in jazz research beyond the cursory remarks of scholars such as Schuller and Berliner. This chapter surveys and categorizes various manifestations of discontinuity, mainly from the middle years of Reinhardt's recorded career, and develops from them a speculative poetics of his improvisational process. I will begin with some clear-cut examples and then progress through cases involving decreasing levels of audible contrast.

Reinhardt hardly ever played a preexisting melody straight through; he usually deferred that responsibility whenever another solo instrument was present, such as Grappelli's violin with the Quintet of the Hot Club of France. On those occasions when he did play a head melody, Reinhardt usually stated it only glancingly, launching into a full-blown improvisation after no more than a few measures. On "In a Sentimental Mood" (4/26/37; mx. OLA 1718-1), after playing an a cappella solo introduction the guitarist states Duke Ellington's melody for only four bars before discarding it. On "Dinah" (12/34; mx. P 77161), from the Quintet's 1934 debut recording session, he improvises for eight bars before invoking the original melody for the next eight-bar section and then dispensing with it again. On "Honeysuckle Rose" (1/31/38; mx. DTB 3523-1) he plays just two bars of Fats Waller's melody to begin his first chorus (see example 5.19), and on "Moonglow" (10/21/35; mx. 2082-HPP) the original melody vanishes after a single bar. Reinhardt was most apt to forgo the melody when playing popular songs that would probably be familiar to listeners of his day. When performing his own compositions he was somewhat more likely to give a literal rendition (though this role, too, was often assigned to a colleague). Rare instances of him giving fairly conservative interpretations of published songs include his recordings of Irving Berlin's "I've Got My Love to Keep Me Warm" (9/1/38; mx. DR 2903-1) and George Gershwin's "The Man I Love" (8/25/39; mx. DR 3864-1). These performances are both duets with Grappelli accompanying on piano, and Reinhardt mainly limits his alterations of each song to rhythmic liberties and subtle ornamental embellishments. Of greater interest here, however, are those occasions when he would play a theme recognizably but also add extensive new material that rises well beyond the level of subordinate ornamentation.

Example 2.2 displays an excerpt from Reinhardt's 1937 recording of "Saint Louis Blues" (9/9/37; mx. OLA 1952-1) with the published melody shown above Reinhardt's rendition. When he arrives at the theme's minor-mode "habanera" section midway through his solo, Reinhardt plays the original theme with a few embellishments. But between each of its phrases he interjects a flamboyant double-time passage, differentiating the familiar melody and the unfamiliar interpolations by register, speed of melodic motion, and also timbre (since he plays the theme on his guitar's lower strings). The discontinuities in this passage are very abrupt: two contrasting musical ideas alternate, creating the illusion of one instrument playing a melody while another plays an obbligato (bracketed in example 2.2). In this way, Reinhardt alone fulfills the two roles that, in performances such as "Studio 24," are split between two different players.

EXAMPLE 2.2. Improvisation on "Saint Louis Blues" (9/9/37; mx. OLA 1952-1). Interpolations between paraphrases of the original melody

In "Saint Louis Blues," Reinhardt adheres closely to the theme as composed, but other solos based on the same alternating process often contain more substantial modifications of the preexisting melody and smoother transitions between the melody and his own contributions. In "If I Had You" (2/1/38; mx. DTB 3532-1), transcribed in example 2.3, Reinhardt mainly interpolates new material toward the end of each original melodic phrase, much as in "Saint Louis Blues." These interpolations grow more extensive as the solo unfolds. The recording, another duet with Grappelli at the piano, opens with Reinhardt stating the written melody (original interpolations are bracketed in example 2.3). The guitar's initial four-bar phrase concludes with a descending improvised gesture that transfers the original melody pitch, D, to a lower octave (m. 1.4), and the next four measures end with an improvised ascending and descending arpeggiation of the underlying harmonies, C♯ diminished-seventh and D minor (with added sixth) (mm. 1.7–1.8). The second eight-bar section is a free but fairly literal rendition of the original tune that concludes with another interpolation (mm. 1.15–1.16). In this solo the contrast between material based on the written melody and improvised interjections is considerably less pronounced than in "Saint Louis Blues," since the discontinuities are not so explicitly projected by differences in register or timbre. They are primarily conceptual and would be most evident to a listener already familiar with the song.

During the bridge of "If I Had You" (mm. 1.17–1.24), Reinhardt consistently transforms the original melody with rhythmic diminutions: in mm. 1.17, 1.19, and 1.21 he halves its note durations, playing the original quarter notes as eighth notes, eighth notes as sixteenth notes, and so forth. This creates more space for his interjections. The bridge's final two and a half measures consist entirely of new material, and after he returns briefly to the original melody in mm. 1.25–1.26 the rest of the chorus's final A section is entirely improvised save for another brief, rhythmically diminished reference to the original theme in m. 1.29.

In both "Saint Louis Blues" and "If I Had You," Reinhardt pursues two concurrent strategies: he interprets a preexisting tune and he improvises new melodic lines that observe only the underlying harmonies. These two solos are fairly atypical, though. Ordinarily, the written melody remains more exclusively confined to his inner consciousness. Only rarely does he briefly state a preexisting theme in the course of an otherwise more fully improvised solo. In such cases, Reinhardt often employs disjunct contrasts with respect to one or more musical parameters (e.g., rhythm, pitch, and texture) so as to highlight the original

Example 2.3. Improvisation on "If I Had You" (2/1/38; mx. DTB 3532-1).
Rhythmic diminution of the original melody, interpolations between
phrases

melody's appearance, as he does on "Saint Louis Blues." Another example of this technique is shown in example 2.4, an excerpt from his second chorus on "Charleston" (4/21/37; mx. OLA 1703-1). Here, at the beginning of the chorus's second eight-bar section (mm. 3.9–3.12), he interrupts his single-string solo by interjecting a (rhythmically altered) paraphrase of the original melody that is highlighted by being played in octaves, creating a sharp discontinuity. In the midst of a highly involved melodic improvisation, this passage serves as a sort of mental guidepost, reminding listeners, and also perhaps, in a confirmatory sense, the performer himself, of the ongoing improvisation's underlying thematic derivation. Reinhardt also uses this technique on his recordings of "Please Be Kind" (9/1/38; mx. DR 2904-1), shortly before the solo ends, and "How High the Moon" (3/26/47; mx. OSW 450-1), at the top of his second chorus.

Thematic paraphrase is clearly a consistent basis for discontinuity in Reinhardt's improvisations. Evidently, the guitarist sometimes draws a conceptual distinction between, on the one hand, interpreting a preexistent melody and, on the other, freer harmonic improvisation, and he emphasizes this distinction, often by reinforcing interjected melodic paraphrases with octave doublings. He even occasionally uses octave doublings when quoting other, unrelated melodies; his 1938 solo on "Honeysuckle Rose" (1/31/38; mx. DTB 3523-1), for instance, references Gershwin's *Rhapsody in Blue* in this way (see example 5.19, mm. 2.12–2.15).

Yet, as seen in "If I Had You," Reinhardt's melodic paraphrases are not always so unequivocally set off from their surroundings. They often appear as subtler references in which conceptual distinctions are not reinforced by audible contrasts. Consider, for instance, his improvisation on "I Can't Give You Anything But Love" (5/4/36; mx. OLA 1058-1), transcribed in example 2.5. Nonbracketed passages of the transcription generally adhere closely to the original melody, though Reinhardt uses many ornamentations and rhythmic alterations such as the diminutions in mm. 1.9–1.10 (similar to those noted in "If I Had You"). The smooth transitions between thematic fragments and free interpolations can blur the distinction between them. For example, the sixteenth-note chords in m. 1.4, which are differentiated texturally (and by their louder volume) from the surrounding monophonic melodic exposition, are also subtly related to the tune. The upper voice of the two alternating chords oscillates between the pitches A♯ and B, which both occur in the original song during this same measure. Similarly, the highest pitches of the final

Example 2.4. Improvisation on "Charleston" (4/21/37; mx. OLA 1703-1). Melodic paraphrase played in octaves

EXAMPLE 2.5. Improvisation on "I Can't Give You Anything But Love" (5/4/36; mx. OLA 1058-1). Integration of melodic paraphrases and free interpolations

Example 2.5. *(cont.)*

chord in m. 1.4 and the succeeding chord on the downbeat of m. 1.5 are respectively B and G, just as in the written theme.

Despite the scope for ambiguity, the distinction between melodic paraphrases and harmonically based improvisation often remains viable. In a 1938 version of "Body and Soul" (5/31/38; mx. CL 6716-1), transcribed in example 2.6, Reinhardt's solo begins in the guitar's upper register with a paraphrase of the melody's opening that inverts its characteristic ascending perfect fifth to become a falling fourth (m. 2.1). In the next few measures the guitarist reverts to a more literal exposition of the melody a full two octaves lower than at first (m. 2.3–2.6). Then, toward the end of the first eight-bar section, he departs from the melody with a double-time excursion of the sort seen in "Saint Louis Blues." Throughout the rest of the solo he continually returns to the written melody's outline; in mm. 2.9–2.10 he isolates it from the double-time elaborative gestures, but elsewhere, such as at the end of m. 2.13

EXAMPLE 2.6. Improvisation on "Body and Soul" (5/31/38; mx. CL 6716-1).
Melodic paraphrases, both integrated and differentiated from free
interpolations, and structural marker, played in octaves, at the solo's
conclusion

(C–A–F), he integrates it seamlessly into the other material. Example 2.6 brackets regions that are not directly based on the original theme. The diminishing level of differentiation between melodic paraphrases and improvised passages found in this solo recalls Cone's concept of synthesis, the process whereby "diverse elements are brought into closer and closer relation with one another."[20] But Cone's formulation also implies a teleological process that is not evident in Reinhardt's improvisation. The melody instead seems to act as a constant mental referent that occasionally is allowed to reappear in various guises.[21]

At the ends of his solos on both "I Can't Give You Anything But Love" and "Body and Soul," Reinhardt employs discontinuity in another way. Rather than differentiating between melodic paraphrases and harmonic improvisation, these discontinuities function to demarcate his theme's underlying form; they create "structural markers" that highlight hypermetrical downbeats (the initial downbeats of the four- or eight-bar units found in conventional jazz song forms).[22] The "Body and Soul" solo ends with an abrupt discontinuity: an ascending five-note gesture played in octaves. This gesture (also bracketed in example 2.6), which is conceptually separate from the main body of the solo, cues the formal boundary between the theme's first sixteen measures and the bridge. In fact, Reinhardt plays an almost identical figure at the same point in the preceding chorus while accompanying harmonica player Larry Adler. Structural markers, often characterized by octave doubling as in the present example, are a recurrent feature of his work as an accompanist. When the same devices occur in his solo improvisations (often producing disjunct contrasts) they have equivalent functions.

A similar structural marker appears toward the end of Reinhardt's 1937 solo on "Solitude" (4/21/37; mx. OLA 1706-1), transcribed in example 2.7. Here it occurs at the improvisation's conclusion, as in the previous example, simultaneously creating a sense of closure and heralding the next instrumental entrance, in this case Grappelli's violin. Because Reinhardt did not engage in much overt musical interaction with his accompanists in the Quintet of the 1930s, he may have been especially inclined to do double duty by supplementing his solos with material that, in other circumstances, could have been played by rhythm section musicians. In a 1936 solo on "Sweet Chorus" (10/15/36; mx. OLA 1295-1), for instance, he interjects incisive chordal statements at two-bar intervals between monophonic passages, suggesting the sort of call-and-response technique described by Lonnie Hillyer (see example 2.8). Much swing era jazz features this sort of interaction between, say, a soloist and an ac-

Example 2.7. Improvisation on "Solitude" (4/21/37; mx. OLA 1706-1).
Structural marker played in octaves

companying pianist or drummer. But the Quintet's rhythm guitarists favored a comparatively undifferentiated, pulsating texture that rarely either directly engaged the soloist or provided aural cues signaling formal boundaries.

Reinhardt uses several of the above described techniques of discontinuity in his 1937 improvisation on "The Sheik of Araby" (4/27/37; mx. OLA 1737-1). This solo (example 2.9) opens in the guitar's upper register with an explicit reference to the beginning of the original melody—the ascending neighbor-note motive F–G. After just two bars Reinhardt shifts abruptly down to his instrument's lowest octave and departs entirely from the published tune for an extended period, through the end of his first chorus. He interrupts this lower-register passage just once, with a seven-note figure, played in octaves, in mm. 3.22–3.24. This abrupt interjection, strikingly incongruent with the surrounding material, can be explained in at least two ways. Because it recalls the original melody by emphasizing the neighbor-note relation, E♭–D (respectively, the flattened ninth and root of the underlying D7 harmony), it implies a loose melodic paraphrase invoking the written melody's climactic moment. Alternatively, given that it occurs just two bars before a hypermetrical downbeat (m. 3.25), it also functions as a structural marker like those in "Body and Soul" and "Solitude." Reinhardt's protracted excursion away from the original melody into the instrument's lower register ends not with a disjunct registral shift, as it began, but with one of his trademark rapid chromatic scales. This virtuosic effect both calls atten-

EXAMPLE 2.8. Improvisation on "Sweet Chorus" (10/15/36; mx. OLA 1295-1). Alternation between chordal figures and single-note melody

tion to and traverses the registral divide between low and high (symbolized in example 2.9 by the use of an oblique line, rather than a closing bracket, to indicate the end of the extended lower-register passage around bar 4.3).

Along with melodic paraphrases and structural markers, a third explanation for discontinuity in Reinhardt's music is the one Hodeir gives in his analysis of "Solid Old Man": the interpolation of accompanimental material. The guitar, like most of jazz's rhythm section instruments,

EXAMPLE 2.9. Improvisation on "The Sheik of Araby" (4/27/37; mx. OLA 1737-1). Melodic paraphrase, structural marker

EXAMPLE 2.9. *(cont.)*

is often played very differently depending on whether it is accompanying or soloing. Solo melodies tend to be primarily monophonic and varied with respect to pitch and rhythm; accompaniments are ordinarily chordal and comparatively homogeneous rhythmically. Sometimes while playing a melodic solo Reinhardt introduces material that is even more explicitly accompanimental than the passage discussed by Hodeir. A clear example occurs on his 1937 recording of "Japanese Sandman" (7/7/37; mx. OLA 1889-1). The performance features members of the Dicky Wells Orchestra with a rhythm section consisting of Reinhardt's guitar plus bassist Dick Fullbright and drummer Bill Beason. This makes for a fairly sparse musical texture when the guitarist solos, so he compensates by strumming chords between phrases of his habitual single-string melodic improvisation (bracketed in example 2.10). This example strongly supports Hodeir's hypothesis that, while Reinhardt was improvising, his mind might have been occupied not only by a fixed referent consisting of his theme's melody and harmonic structure but also by an associated accompanimental "background" texture.[23] When realized as a repetitive, ostinato-like pattern, this conceptual background both thickens the music's texture and sustains the rhythmic momentum during lulls between guitar phrases belonging to the musical foreground. The effect is of simultaneous progression: the background material remains conceptually present even when it is aurally absent.[24]

Reinhardt's adeptness at switching swiftly between background rhythmic figures, melodic paraphrases, and straightforward foreground improvisation, even at very fast tempi, is evident at the start of his 1935 solo on "I've Had My Moments" (9/35; mx. P 77538), shown in example

EXAMPLE 2.10. Improvisation on "Japanese Sandman" (7/7/37; mx. OLA 1889-1). Interpolated accompanimental chords

2.11. The solo's first five bars contain a reiterated eighth-note G♮ followed by a series of strummed chords. This passage's character is strongly accompanimental, contrasting sharply with the material that follows (mm. 2.5–2.9).[25] Even the initial, nonchordal reiterated open G string is differentiated from the succeeding paraphrase simply by its repetitive, uniform pitch content; like the chords that follow, it heightens the sense of a dynamic, propulsive accompanimental groove. At m. 2.5, Reinhardt abruptly shifts to an embellished paraphrase of the published melody (shown above the transcription), and he does not begin playing more fully improvised melodic phrases until five bars later, in m. 2.10.

Along the same lines, the series of eighth notes in mm. 2.32–3.4 can also be designated an accompaniment-like passage. This interpretation is more tenuous than the previous one because, while this second passage is also quite repetitive (and, like the earlier passage, has a heightened sense of momentum due to the cross-rhythms produced by accenting every third note), Reinhardt introduces several other pitches after beginning with only E♮. Nonetheless, aside from the final B♮s (m. 3.4), the passage's melodic profile is markedly different from that of the preceding measures.[26] Reinhardt often uses such repetitive single-note patterns around the beginning of a new chorus; another example is the second take of his 1947 improvisation on "Babik (Bi-Bop)" (5/21/47; mx. Fo 1785-RC). They may also serve as intellectual-labor-saving devices, making it easier for him to keep playing while gathering inspiration for more involved subsequent activity.

In the previous two examples, selected musical material has been designated part of an improvisation's background largely because it is relatively homogeneous. A musical accompaniment can, however, be distinguishable from a primary melody without being comparatively repetitive. A pianist's irregular comping and a drummer's sporadic interjections on a snare or bass drum are, for instance, often integral elements of an interactive jazz rhythm section as it supports an improvising soloist. In larger ensembles, such as swing era big bands, soloists may be accompanied by instrumental backgrounds, riffs, and send-offs. Reinhardt sometimes creates equivalent sorts of musical discontinuity by inserting rifflike material within a single-note solo. This additional discontinuous practice can be considered another sort of background-oriented technique.

Reinhardt often juxtaposes short, chordal, rifflike fragments against monophonic melodies, usually with symmetrical metric groupings, as il-

EXAMPLE 2.11. Improvisation on "I've Had My Moments" (5/35; mx. P77538). Accompanimental background, melodic paraphrase

EXAMPLE 2.11. *(cont.)*

47

Example 2.11. *(cont.)*

lustrated in example 2.12, which contains excerpts from two takes of his 1939 recording of "Jeepers Creepers" (3/21/39; mx. 4968-1/2HPP and 4968-HPP). A comparison between the alternate take and the master suggests that the rifflike material on the master might have been, like background figuration or melodic paraphrases, more premeditated than the guitarist's customary single-note solo melodies. Likewise, while the two takes are in many ways dissimilar, they both contain a passage played in octaves during the final bridge of each solo (bracketed toward the ends of examples 2.12b and 2.12d), so this discontinuous effect might also have been somewhat preplanned. Reinhardt's a cappella guitar introduction to the alternate take, which was recorded first, begins with a harmonized reference to the published melody, D–C–C–B♭ (example 2.12a). At m. 3.9 of his solo on the same take, shown in example 2.12b, he plays a descending melodic sequence of arpeggiated triads that culminates in a chordal figure (m. 3.11–3.12); he continues in mm.

3.13–3.16 with a four-bar passage, mainly in three-part chords, whose upper voice begins with the semitonal motion D–C♯–C–C♯–D (bracketed in the transcription). The latter chordal motive, which he may well have conceived spontaneously, is then used as the basis for the introduction to the second take, subsequently designated the master, which would probably have been recorded only minutes after the alternate version (see example 2.12c). Reinhardt then reintroduces the same motive a third time in m. 3.9 of his solo on the master take, approximately where it first appeared on the earlier take (example 2.12d). He now uses it as the first of a pair of two-bar chordal interjections—another variant appears in m. 3.13—that alternate with monophonic passages, an effect reminiscent of big band call-and-response exchanges between a soloist and an ensemble.

In big band arrangements of the swing era, these sorts of short, rifflike ensemble passages often function as send-offs at the beginning of a chorus or other significant formal division, punctuating an improvised solo. In the same way, Reinhardt sometimes interjects brief send-off-like statements, generally two or four bars long and played in chords or octaves, at the start of a formal section. Example 2.13, an excerpt from his 1949 solo on "Marie" (1–2/49; mx. CW 38), shows one such instance (mm. 3.1–3.4), played in octaves at the top of a new chorus. These devices may, at the same time, function as structural markers, though they differ from the more common instances of such devices in that they usually *begin* on or around the first downbeat of a new formal unit, whereas more explicit structural markers tend to *end* approximately on (or slightly before) the hypermetrical downbeat.

In most of the examples discussed so far, Reinhardt's use of musical discontinuity involves some combination of conceptual and literal differentiation. To summarize, conceptual distinctions exist between (1) material that paraphrases a theme's preexisting melody, (2) material derived mainly from the improviser's own improvisational language (musical formulas, spontaneous invention, and so forth), and (3) accompaniment-like passages that may include devices functioning as structural markers. The conceptual distinction between background (accompanimental) and foreground material is very often linked to literal differentiation; background material tends to feature a repetitive rhythmic groove or chordal interjections, both of which sharply contrast with the single-line melodies that make up the bulk of Reinhardt's solos. References to an original melody are less strongly linked to literal differentiation because a theme can be invoked simply by paraphrasing it without

EXAMPLE 2.12a. Improvisation on "Jeepers Creepers" (3/21/39; mx. 4968-1/2HPP). Solo guitar chordal introduction on the first (alternate) take

EXAMPLE 2.12b. Improvisation on "Jeepers Creepers" (3/21/39; mx. 4968-1/2HPP). Chordal passage during the guitar solo on the first (alternate) take

Example 2.12c. Improvisation on "Jeepers Creepers" (3/21/39; mx. 4968-HPP). Solo guitar introduction on the second (master) take based on the chordal passage from the first take

Example 2.12d. Improvisation on "Jeepers Creepers" (3/21/39; mx. 4968-HPP). Recurrence of the introductory material during the guitar solo on the second (master) take

EXAMPLE 2.13. Improvisation on "Marie" (1–2/49; mx. CW 38). Send-off-like interjection at the start of a new chorus played in octaves

necessarily reinforcing the conceptual distinction by, for example, playing in octaves.

It is worth noting that background material, differentiated from its surroundings by means of register, texture, or motivic content, does not always function simply as a contrasting supplement to the foreground. Occasionally it contains motivic development of its own, as occurs in a fairly lengthy excursion toward the background during Reinhardt's 1939 solo on "H.C.Q. Strut" (8/25/39; mx. DR 3862-1). This simple theme features a repetitive bass line that descends chromatically from scale degree #4 through scale degree 3, underpinning a V/V–V7–I harmonic progression. The melody and bass line of the tune's A section are shown in example 2.14a. (The bassist on the recording, Emmanuel Soudieux, plays this line with little variation.) Two bars into his solo's second chorus (m. 3.3 in example 2.14b), Reinhardt switches abruptly from an elaborate arpeggiated foreground melody to a figure derived from the underlying bass line. Although this passage does not exhibit the sort of repetitive figuration that is typically associated with accompanimental material in Reinhardt's music, it can still be designated a background figure in that it is directly related to the theme's underlying bass progression.[27] At first Reinhardt doubles the bass pitches an octave

EXAMPLE 2.14a. "H.C.Q. Strut," original melody and bass line

EXAMPLE 2.14b. Improvisation on "H.C.Q. Strut" (8/25/39; mx. DR 3862-1). Background passage based on the original bass line

higher and adds another note, a minor seventh above each bass-doubling note. The resultant motive, which sharply contrasts with all that precedes it, is soon transformed into a three-note ascending gesture that he develops over the next ten measures. Then, just as abruptly, he reverts to foreground mode (m. 3.13), giving the impression of resuming where he left off. During this interlude, which is clearly inspired by the tune's bass line and out of character with the surrounding upper-register melodic activity, Reinhardt remains creatively involved with the solo's background long enough to give it some variety rather than treating it as comparatively homogeneous (in the manner of examples 2.10 and 2.11).

All told, the foregoing examples suggest that discontinuous regions of Reinhardt's solos are often manifestations of different strata of his subjective consciousness. The guitarist's predominant mode of improvisation involves creating new melodic material. But he conceives this foregrounded material with reference to a harmonic structure that ordinarily supports a melody, and from time to time this melody—usually consigned to his inner consciousness—becomes explicit, often in a way that sets it off from the surrounding passages. He also appears to sustain an inner image of the passing harmonies in the form of a repetitive rhythmic ostinato.[28] This accompanimental background also sometimes becomes explicit, often functioning to provide structural markers; create chordal, rifflike exchanges; supplement a sparse musical accompaniment; or keep the music going while he gathers inspiration.

Although clear-cut discontinuities occur in many of Reinhardt's recorded solos, they are not the norm. More often paraphrases of a written theme are fairly smoothly integrated with original melodies and background figuration without audible discontinuities (along the lines of "If I Had You" [example 2.3] and "Body and Soul" [example 2.6]). Yet given the ample evidence of Reinhardt's tendency to differentiate between separate conceptual strata, it is sometimes possible to discern the same sorts of conceptual distinctions even when audible discontinuities are less immediately perceptible. When doing so there is, of course, always a risk of imposing inflexible categorical distinctions on ambiguous passages, as noted earlier in "I Can't Give You Anything But Love" (example 2.5), but this risk is often offset by interpretive insights. To illustrate, I now offer some closing remarks on two complete solos that encapsulate the musical issues discussed in this chapter: "Bricktop" (1–2/49; mx. CW 56) and "Liza" (2/1/46; mx. DR 10029-1).

Example 2.15 is a transcription of Reinhardt's 1949 solo on "Bricktop" with the notation distributed across three staves. The lowest staff contains musical material that I have designated as belonging to the improvisation's background level. This includes not only repetitive accompaniment-like figures, but also send-off riffs and structural markers (these could themselves be divided between three separate staves, but they have been grouped together for the sake of simplicity). The middle staff is reserved for all passages that paraphrase part of the original melody at approximately its original location in the piece's form. (In this solo only one such paraphrase occurs; since the middle staff is otherwise redundant it is shown only at the very beginning and toward the end of the transcription in mm. 3.15–3.21.) The top staff holds everything else, which is to say all foreground musical material with no obvious connection to the original melody.

"Bricktop," which features Reinhardt with a rhythm section of piano, bass, and drums, is among the last recordings he made on the acoustic guitar before deciding to concentrate more or less exclusively on the electric instrument. The theme consists solely of a repeating eight-bar phrase. On the recording this phrase is played four times as a thirty-two-bar opening head statement, but Reinhardt's improvisation is seventy-two measures long; it has been transcribed (essentially arbitrarily) as one forty-bar chorus followed by another of thirty-two bars. Much of the guitar solo involves alternations between contrasting material approximately every four bars or so, creating a sense of strict periodicity. Figure 2.1 summarizes the scheme set out in example 2.15. Reinhardt opens his solo with sixteen bars of foreground single-note melodic improvisation (labeled "F.G." in fig. 2.1) and then inserts the first of three four-bar chordal send-off riffs. Twelve more bars of foregrounded material follow; the only other uninterrupted passage of similar length occurs at the solo's end. The four-bar send-offs usually comprise two slightly different statements of basically the same two-bar motive; they are each followed by a four-bar phrase containing a falling melodic contour that arrives on the tonic note, G♮. The initial send-off somewhat re-

\\	1st Chorus (40 mm.)				\\			2nd Chorus (32 mm.)			\\
16	+ 4	+ 12	+ 4	+ 4	+ 4	+ 4	+ 4	+ 4	+ 4	+ 12	
F.G.	Riff	F.G.	Riff	F.G.	Riff	F.G.	Bgrnd.	F.G.	Mldy.	F.G.	
	m. 2.17		m. 2.33		m. 3.1		m. 3.9		m. 3.17		

FIG. 2.1. Overview of "Bricktop"

sembles the melody (m. 2.17), but the clearest melodic paraphrase comes with the final discontinuous insertion (m. 3.17), as if to counterbalance the earlier one. The repeated eighth-note A♮s beginning at m. 3.9 are the only explicitly accompaniment-like interpolation (i.e., not a send-off).

Example 2.16 is a transcription of Reinhardt's solo on "Liza," distributed, like the previous example, across three staves: background, melodic paraphrases, and foreground. Above these staves is a fourth staff, which displays the melody as originally published; the song is a thirty-two-bar AABA form. Reinhardt punctuates his solo, which contains relatively few explicit discontinuities, with a four-bar melodic paraphrase at the beginning of the final A section during all three of his choruses (mm. 2.25, 3.25, and 4.25); these paraphrases all start with a G♮ that dovetails with a preceding melodic line. In the first chorus (mm. 2.23–2.24) the linear progression C–B–A precedes the paraphrase, and in the third chorus another descent, from E♭, is heard (m. 4.24); in the second chorus an ascending chromatic scale culminates with the same pitch G (mm. 3.23–3.24). Example 2.16 also indicates that Reinhardt's improvisation contains six different background ostinato figures (mm. 2.5–2.8, 3.9–3.12, 3.30–4.3, 4.7–4.9, 4.22–4.24, and 4.30–4.32). The third of these (mm. 3.30–4.3) straddles the initial downbeat of a new thirty-two-bar chorus, deemphasizing this formal boundary and thus counteracting the overall strong periodicity of the solo, which is heavily based on four-bar phrases. In contrast, the beginning of Reinhardt's second chorus (m. 3.1) is marked by an emphatic four-measure send-off-like pattern played in octaves.

Ed Sarath's theory of the cognitive psychology of musical improvisation sheds some light on Reinhardt's creative process in "Liza."[29] Sarath depicts spontaneous creation as arising from mental "cognitive event cycles."[30] Each cognitive event cycle consists of a player receiving perceptual data (stemming from both external sounds and the silent inner presence of the theme) and then choosing a strategy for continuing the improvisation.[31] The higher the frequency of these cognitive event cycles the better able he or she will be to execute fresh strategies conceived "in the moment." Conversely, the slower their frequency the more likely it is that the improviser will use repetition, or preestablished material, whether it be drawn from his or her own repertoire of melodic formulas or from elements of the theme itself.[32] Sarath's model resonates with the testimony of some jazz improvisers, including the saxophonist Lee Konitz, who has described his improvisatory process in terms of a series of conceptual levels ranging from noncreative replication of a theme

EXAMPLE 2.15. Improvisation on "Bricktop" (1–2/49; mx. CW 56).
Foreground, melodic paraphrase, and background

57

EXAMPLE 2.15. *(cont.)*

EXAMPLE 2.15. *(cont.)*

EXAMPLE 2.15. *(cont.)*

EXAMPLE 2.15. *(cont.)*

EXAMPLE 2.16. Improvisation on "Liza" (2/1/46; mx. DR 10029-1).
Foreground, melodic paraphrase, and background

EXAMPLE 2.16. *(cont.)*

EXAMPLE 2.16. *(cont.)*

EXAMPLE 2.16. *(cont.)*

EXAMPLE 2.16. *(cont.)*

EXAMPLE 2.16. *(cont.)*

EXAMPLE 2.16. *(cont.)*

EXAMPLE 2.16. *(cont.)*

EXAMPLE 2.16. *(cont.)*

EXAMPLE 2.16. *(cont.)*

EXAMPLE 2.16. *(cont.)*

through increasing degrees of embellishment to "the creation of wholly new melodies."[33]

Drawing on Sarath's and Konitz's observations, we can view Reinhardt's performance of "Liza" as shifting between different "creative levels." Repetitive background material may indicate a relatively low creative level, a slow rate of cognitive event cycles in Sarath's terms; embellished, or otherwise slightly modified, expressions of the preexistent melody imply a somewhat greater creative level; and original, spontaneously conceived material of comparative complexity may represent a still higher level of mental activity. Thinking of jazz improvisation in terms of these levels—which are, naturally, loose interpretative metaphors rather than rigorously quantifiable objective categories—highlights the music's underlying dynamic human cognitive processes rather than the audible structures that these processes generate. (It should, as an aside, be noted that in some ways Sarath's and Konitz's perspectives differ significantly. Sarath construes his model of the improvisational process as a value hierarchy: a higher rate of cognitive event cycles implies a greater "creative potential" and is thus regarded as a "creative goal."[34] Konitz, by contrast, takes the view that "no one level is more important than any other," an attitude I share.[35] In referring to "higher" or "lower" creative levels, I am not making any value judgments.)

After beginning his solo on "Liza" with an eight-bar stretch of relatively complex melodic invention, Reinhardt introduces background material in mm. 2.5–2.8, implying a momentary period of reduced creative activity whose repetitive pitch content enables him to devote more attention to planning the forthcoming foregrounded material that begins at m. 2.9. The rest of the improvisation can be interpreted along similar lines. In this particular solo, certain melodic patterns often recur with only small modifications (compare, e.g., mm. 2.15–2.16 with mm. 2.31–2.32 or mm. 3.5–3.8 with mm. 3.13–3.16), which suggests that they may derive from Reinhardt's personal vocabulary of melodic formulas. Alternatively, these sorts of comparatively invariant melodic ideas may be specific to this occasion, and as such they could have been prepared shortly beforehand or invented in the course of the performance. Irrespective of their actual derivation, their recurrence suggests a creative level somewhat beneath that of nonrepeated foregrounded passages—such as the diverse material introduced at the beginning of each chorus's bridge (mm. 2.17, 3.17, 4.17)—whose uniqueness implies that they are more spontaneously conceived. These sorts of speculations will be better informed once we know more about the guitarist's customary formulaic vocabulary, which the next chapter addresses.

I believe that, at the very least, the radically discontinuous character of Reinhardt's music is not an analytical obstacle to be either surmounted or circumvented but is worth considering in and of itself. (Conversely, this chapter has intentionally bypassed questions regarding structural unity.) Whether or not the theoretical framework developed here can be fruitfully applied to the work of other jazz improvisers is, however, an open question. While the sort of "dissection" performed on "Bricktop" and "Liza" might readily be carried out on solos by other jazz musicians, this could easily lead to highly arbitrary parsings. In examples 2.15 and 2.16, I can only justify my interpretation of discontinuities as signaling the performer's mental shifts of attention between foreground improvisation, melodic paraphrases, and repetitive background patterns because Reinhardt elsewhere makes these conceptual distinctions far more explicitly. One reason why these distinctions are often so sharp is that, as noted, the guitar, like all rhythm section instruments, is conventionally played very differently when the performer is soloing (playing single-note lines) than when he or she is accompanying (strumming chords), and these associations persist in other contexts. But improvised discontinuities that imply a process of shifting between different psychological strata can be associated with any instrument, and the case of Louis Armstrong's vocal technique, as well as Berliner's account of horn players who simulate call-and-response-type phrases, raises the possibility that the framework set forth here may have broader applications.

One of this chapter's basic observations—that the chordal and octave-doubled passages that Reinhardt often inserts within his solos are, by and large, more invariant than the monophonic material that surrounds them—broaches a more general question: in what respects do the guitarist's improvisations involve preestablished material and strategies? The next chapter delves further into this issue by investigating melodic formulas, the recurrent licks and phrases that are an essential ingredient of any improviser's musical language.

❂ 3 ❂
FORMULAIC IMPROVISATION

Just as people continually reuse various words and phrases in everyday conversation, improvising musicians draw on their own vocabularies of stock devices, commonly called "formulas," when playing. This chapter compiles a taxonomy of Reinhardt's personal formulas and analyzes their use in selected solos. Research in this field has, in recent decades, taken as its starting point an influential hypothesis proposed by the classicists Milman Parry and Albert Lord about how the Homeric epics originated.[1] Based on their observation of illiterate Serbo-Croatian storytellers of the 1930s, these two scholars theorized that the *Odyssey* and *Iliad* were initially created and transmitted by oral poets who wove together a variety of reusable "association[s] of sounds, words, phrases, and lines" that Parry and Lord termed "formulas."[2] Musical improvisation works in a similar way.[3]

The first writer to thoroughly investigate the use of musical formulas in jazz was Thomas Owens in a monumental 1974 dissertation on the bebop saxophonist Charlie Parker. After examining a large number of transcribed solos, Owens compiled a list of sixty-four of Parker's favored formulas (which he called "motives"), tallied how frequently each occurred, and determined that Parker associated some of them with specific keys (probably because, unlike the guitar, the saxophone generally requires different fingerings for transpositions of the same material, so some formulas fall most readily under the hands in particular keys).[4] He also noted that Parker consistently used certain formulas at similar points within a tune's form regardless of the particular tune the saxophonist was playing.

Subsequent authors who adapted Parry and Lord's theory to jazz include Lawrence Gushee, Barry Kernfeld, and Gregory Smith, who wrote in the early 1980s on the music of Lester Young, John Coltrane, and Bill Evans, respectively.[5] Gushee's 1981 article on Young's 1936–37 recordings of the tune "Shoe Shine Boy" distinguished between "formulas," whose appearance remains fairly consistent from one occurrence to the next, and "superformulas," which vary more widely, a distinction that will prove useful with respect to Reinhardt's music.[6] One of Kernfeld's chief aims in his study of Coltrane was to explain how separate formulas can interrelate within larger melodic networks, a topic that the second half of this chapter will address in relation to some complete improvisations.[7]

Owens and Gushee were fairly inexplicit about their criteria for identifying melodic formulas, but Kernfeld and Smith both addressed this thorny issue directly. Kernfeld opted for flexibility, simply requiring that to qualify as a formula a melodic pattern must be "distinctive" from "commonplace rhythms, harmonic implications, or intervallic contours."[8] Smith, by contrast, sought to define formulas precisely based on strict criteria of melodic contour.[9] One upshot was that he classified certain melodic patterns (with similar pitch contours) as instances of the same formula even though they were so radically dissimilar rhythmically that it is unlikely the other authors would have labeled them alike.[10] The issue remains intractable simply because improvisers generally use formulas in unsystematic ways that are not well suited to highly rigorous classification. For practical purposes, this chapter therefore adopts a flexible approach that yields richer, if less definitive, insights than would be possible under more stringent conditions.

Further issues germane to the present study have been raised by two scholars, Howard Spring and Jonathan Finkelman, writing on the guitarist Charlie Christian's use of improvisational formulas. Spring takes harmonic context into account, noting that Christian tended to associate certain formulas with a tonic chord and others with nontonic harmonies; he also, like Kernfeld, explores how various formulas can be combined into larger units.[11] Finkelman reconceptualizes formulas "not as isolated ideas, but instead as recurring patterns that arise from underlying modes of operating and thinking."[12] He divides Christian's formulas into four categories according to their basic fingering configurations, determining the fingerings speculatively, and then uses tablature notation to illustrate how certain groups of notes fall readily under the fingers at various positions on the guitar fretboard (with respect to the prevailing key). Although Reinhardt's specific fingerings are not central to the present chapter, technical issues have been a consideration when categorizing his formulaic vocabulary. Additional present criteria for classification include the formulas' degree of variability, their length, how they function collectively, and whether they appear in consistent formal locations.

The term *formulaic* is often used pejoratively to mean hackneyed and unoriginal, and some observers have accordingly characterized jazz artists' use of musical formulas—often called licks or clichés—as a shortcoming even if it is to some extent inevitable.[13] I do not share this view. I regard musical formulas as an inherent component of any improviser's craft—as a practical necessity and by no means an artistic defect. To be sure, insofar as originality and imagination are widely considered musical virtues, an improviser who heavily relies on a limited number of melodic formulas might well be considered mediocre, but such a judgment would indicate an aesthetic bias against repetition, not against formulas per se.

This chapter's taxonomy of Reinhardt's formulas is drawn from approximately two hundred transcriptions from his recordings and identifies forty-one different melodic patterns.[14] The list should not be regarded as complete or definitive; it is based on a limited selection of Reinhardt's nine-hundred-plus discs, which of course document only a tiny fraction of the music he played in his lifetime.[15] Since the formulas have been identified by subjective, unsystematic criteria, it might well be possible to find more of them within the present sample itself. What follows is simply a starting point offering some practical solutions to some of the methodological problems noted above.

All of the recurrent melodic figures that I have classified as formulas contain at least four notes. Reinhardt tends, on the whole, to reuse numerous melodic devices without rigorous consistency; certain patterns continually reappear with recognizable similarities but slight intervallic and rhythmic modifications. Still, one basic categorical distinction arises: while the guitarist treats most recurrent figures quite freely, some of them tend to be far less changeable than the rest. The former are here designated "variable" formulas; the latter are characterized as "stable." This distinction is a broad generalization, for the boundary between stable and variable formulas can be blurred and even the most stable melodic patterns are sometimes altered within a comparatively narrow range of possibilities.[16] Here the physical aspect of Reinhardt's playing is relevant. Stable formulas are for the most part highly guitaristic: they exploit the instrument's specific technical capabilities, often involving open strings or employing fingerings that fall readily under the hand. The derivation of variable formulas is, conversely, more conceptual than physical. Left-hand fingerings have thus been taken into consideration, although they are not used as a primary basis for categorizing the formulas as in Finkelman's study of Charlie Christian.

The following list groups together formulas that have features in common. In some cases, Reinhardt associates short melodic units with various consistent prefix and suffix figures along the lines of the combinatorial procedures discussed by Spring in Christian's playing or the larger-scale melodic cell families that Kernfeld identifies in Coltrane's improvisations. The given list also includes several comparatively long formulas that consist of strings of shorter formulas. (The constituent shorter formulas are assigned separate labels because they often occur independently, too.) The longer formulas are here designated "superformulas," although I use the term in a rather different sense from Gushee's. Gushee's superformulas are more variable than average, while the same term here describes fairly invariant (stable) configurations (indeed, they are more stable than their constituent formulas tend to be in other contexts).[17]

Reinhardt consistently uses certain formulas at specific points within the forms of the themes on which he improvises regardless of the particular piece he is playing (the same phenomenon that Owens has noted in Parker's improvisations). I call these formulas "context specific." Most of them occur at or near a significant structural boundary such as the initial downbeat of a new chorus; some are usually heard in the few measures preceding such a boundary, and others typically begin at the hypermetrical downbeat itself. Context-specific formulas tend to take a variety of forms and so can additionally be classified as variable.

Before proceeding further it is worth raising an issue that will be discussed at length in this book's final chapter: Reinhardt's stylistic evolution over the course of his career. Studies of formulaic improvisation in music have generally been conceived synchronically, either because they deal only with a brief snapshot of an artist's career (such as the work of Gushee and Kernfeld) or because they treat a performer's style as essentially unchanging throughout the period under consideration (Owens makes this claim with regard to Parker's playing).[18] However, Reinhardt's style changed significantly over time, and so did his habitual formulaic vocabulary. Recordings document the gradual drift of various melodic patterns into and out of his playing as the years passed. A number of superformulas, for instance, seem to have coalesced during the mid-1940s, just over a decade into his mature recorded career, around the time when he became interested in bebop. Although he used most of his formulas consistently enough to justify a basically synchronic perspective here, stylistic changes will sometimes be noted.

In summary, Reinhardt's repertory of formulas are categorized as follows.

(1) Variable formulas: the most common type, and quite changeable in their appearances
(2) Stable formulas: less changeable, and often highly idiomatic to the guitar
(3) Superformulas (stable): significantly longer than average, and often comprising a number of shorter, variable formulas
(4) Context-specific formulas (variable): consistently occurring at certain formal locations regardless of the piece being played

Figure 3.1 displays representative examples of each formula identified by tune, recording date, and measure number. In many cases I give several different examples of the same formula (labeled a, b, c, and so forth) so as to illustrate the range of melodic patterns that have been classified together on the basis of shared features. Lead-sheet-style chord symbols and their corresponding Roman numerals indicate the harmonic context in which Reinhardt played each selected formula. The given key signatures are of little consequence since, owing to the guitar's inherent ease of transposition, Reinhardt's formulas are not key specific except for those stable formulas that involve open strings. Likewise, the given durational values are relative. So, for instance, if Reinhardt plays in double time (as he often does at slow tempos), a particular formula will be notated with its rhythmic values halved (e.g., compare the two examples in F1a). Since Reinhardt often plays the same formulas in many different metric locations (i.e., starting anywhere within a given bar), bar lines have been omitted from the figure.

◎ VARIABLE FORMULAS ◎

Formulas 1–19 are variable. The first three each contain a descending arpeggio.

Variable Formulas

Fɪɢ. 3.1. Reinhardt's melodic formulas

FIG. 3.1. *(cont.)*

F5

a) D (I)

b) B♭ (I)

c) D (I)   C♯m7(♭5) (VII)

"Moonglow"
(10/21/35), 1.15

"I Got Rhythm"
(1-2/49), 3.9

"Them There Eyes"
(6/14/38), 2.2

F6

B7 (V7/II)

"My Sweet" (1/31/38), 3.11

F7

B♭ (I)

"Hangin' Around
Boudon" (7/7/37), 2.7

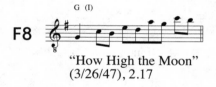

F8

G (I)

"How High the Moon"
(3/26/47), 2.17

F9

F (I)   C7 (V7)

"Honeysuckle Rose"
(1/31/38), 1.8

Fɪɢ. 3.1. *(cont.)*

F10

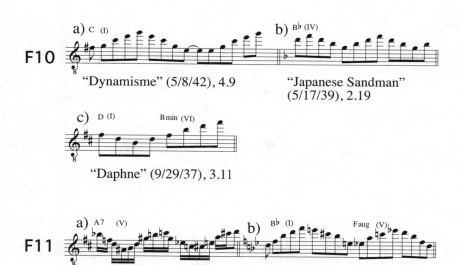

a) C (I)

"Dynamisme" (5/8/42), 4.9

b) B♭ (IV)

"Japanese Sandman" (5/17/39), 2.19

c) D (I)   Bmin (VI)

"Daphne" (9/29/37), 3.11

F11

a) A7 (V)

"A Little Love, A Little Kiss" (4/26/37), 3.5

b) B♭ (I)   Faug (V)

"Hot Lips" (4/22/37), 2.7

c) B♭ (I)

"Blue Light Blues" (3/7/38), 7.6

d) D (I)   A7 (V)

"Ain't Misbehavin'" (4/22/37), 3.29

F12

a) C (I)

"Three Little Words" (6/14/38), 2.26

b) D7 (V7/II)

"Avalon" (7/35), 3.27

c) A7 (V7)

"Coquette" (1/31/46), 2.4

d) Dmin (II)

"Tornerai" (2/1/38), 4.12

e) G7 (V7/IV)

"Nagasaki" (10/15/36), 1.5

f) E♭7 (bVI7)

"Stompin' at Decca" (1/31/38), 2.4

Fɪɢ. 3.1. *(cont.)*

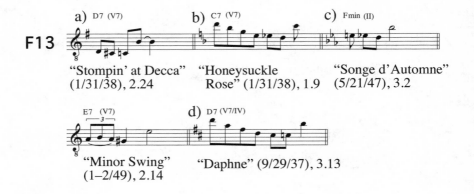

F13

a) D7 (V7)

"Stompin' at Decca"
(1/31/38), 2.24

b) C7 (V7)

"Honeysuckle
Rose" (1/31/38), 1.9

c) Fmin (II)

"Songe d'Automne"
(5/21/47), 3.2

E7 (V7)

"Minor Swing"
(1–2/49), 2.14

d) D7 (V7/IV)

"Daphne" (9/29/37), 3.13

F14

a) F7 (IV7)

"Festival Swing"
(12/26/40), 12.5

b) Bmin (III) B♭dim (bIII)

"I Wonder Where
My Baby is Tonight"
(5/17/39). 4.25

c) F♯min (II)

"My Melancholy
Baby" (3/22/39), 3.6

F15

a) G7 (V7)

"Blues Clair"
(2/26/43), 1.9

b) Amin (I)

"Minor Swing"
(11/25/37), 3.2

c) B♭ (I)

"Charleston" (4/21/37), 3.1

d) Dmin (II)

"Ol' Man River"
(11/14/47), 2.9

F16

C (I)

"R-Vingt Six" (3/26/47), 2.5

FIG. 3.1. *(cont.)*

F17

"Blue Lou" (3/26/47), 2.1

F18

a) "A Little Love,
A Little Kiss"
(4/26/37), 3.4

b) "My Sweet" (1/31/38), 2.20

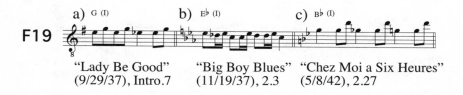

F19

a) "Lady Be Good"
(9/29/37), Intro.7

b) "Big Boy Blues"
(11/19/37), 2.3

c) "Chez Moi a Six Heures"
(5/8/42), 2.27

Stable Formulas

F20

"Limehouse Blues" (5/4/36), 4.11

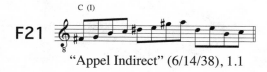

F21

"Appel Indirect" (6/14/38), 1.1

Fig. 3.1. *(cont.)*

F22

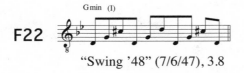

"Swing '48" (7/6/47), 3.8

F23

"Exactly Like You" (4/21/37), 2.1   "Dinah" (12/34), 2.25

F24

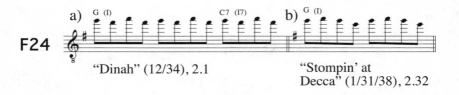

"Dinah" (12/34), 2.1   "Stompin' at
Decca" (1/31/38), 2.32

F25

"I've Had My
Moments" (9/35), 2.17   "Solitude" (4/21/37), 2.27

F26

"Limehouse Blues"
(5/4/36), 5.13

Fɪɢ. 3.1. *(cont.)*

"Nagasaki" (10/15/36), 1.23   "Love's Melody" (2/1/46), 2.8

"Confessin'" (3/10/53), 3.10

"Just One of Those Things" (5/21/47), 2.43

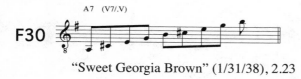

"Sweet Georgia Brown" (1/31/38), 2.23

"Confessin'" (3/35), 2.23

"Lady Be Good" (12/4/34), 2.25

Fig. 3.1. *(cont.)*

Superformulas

F32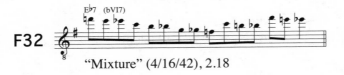

"Mixture" (4/16/42), 2.18

F33

"Japanese Sandman" (5/17/39), 3.18

F34

"Porto Cabello" (5/21/47), 1.17

"Hungaria" (take 1) (3/21/39), 5.13

F35

"Anniversary Song"   "Distraction" (4/16/42), 2.23
(7/6/47), 2.9

"Dynamisme" (5/8/42), 4.13 "Coquette" (1/31/46), 2.12

FIG. 3.1. *(cont.)*

F36 "Ol' Man River" (11/14/47), 2.1

F37 a) "Marie" (1-2/49), 3.5

b) "Confessin'" (3/10/53), 3.12

Context-Specific formulas

F38 a) "Exactly Like You" (4/21/37), 3.23

b) "Ain't Misbehavin'" (4/22/37), 2.25

c) "My Melancholy Baby" (3/22/39), 2.30

d) "Daphne" (1/31/38), 3.30

e) "Ain't Misbehavin'" (4/22/37), 2.7

FIG. 3.1. *(cont.)*

"Hot Lips" (4/22/37), 2.30

"It Had to Be You"
(2/1/38), 2.5

"Rose Room" (4/22/37), 2.20

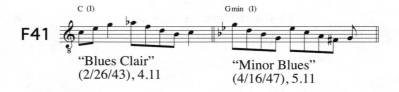

"Blues Clair"
(2/26/43), 4.11

"Minor Blues"
(4/16/47), 5.11

FIG. 3.1. *(cont.)*

F1: A downward four-note arpeggio consisting of two eighth notes followed by two quarters (F1a–c) or, less frequently, of two eighths between two quarters (F1d). It usually begins on a downbeat and often appears at the end of a phrase. F1 commonly arpeggiates a root-position triad (such as in F1a) but may also express a 6-4 inversion (as in F1b from "Runnin' Wild" [4/26/37; mx. OLA 1712-1]) or end with two iterations of the same pitch (F1c).

F2: A descending step followed by a descending arpeggio. The exact intervallic content varies; the step may be a whole or half step, and the arpeggio may be any type of triad. The different versions shown illustrate Reinhardt's propensity to use similar melodic patterns in different harmonic contexts. F2a can appear as the third, ninth, seventh, and fifth of an underlying dominant-seventh harmony ("A Little Love, A Little Kiss" [4/26/37; mx. OLA 1716-1]) or as the sixth, fifth, third, and root of a minor harmony ("Three Little Words" [6/14/38; mx. 4212-HPP]). F2c, an arpeggiation of a half-diminished-seventh (or minor with added sixth) chord, appears with identical pitch content (A–G–E♭–C) over both a D7 harmony ("The Sunshine of Your Smile" [4/35; mx. P 77353]) and a C-minor harmony ("Sweet Chorus" [10/15/36; mx. OLA 1295-1]). This sort of variability is typical. In F2e the formula is preceded by a turn ornamentation, a typical prefix device of Reinhardt's (see F15).

F3: A descending pentatonic scale segment. Certain instances of F2 may be nonstepwise pentatonic subsets (e.g, F2d). F3 designates a descending pentatonic configuration that does not contain an explicit arpeggiated triad of the sort identified as F2.

Formulas 4–6 all involve some form of ascending arpeggiation.

F4: A rising arpeggiation of a diminished-seventh harmony. This is one of the most common formulas in Reinhardt's improvisations; it often occurs with either of two suffixes: (1) upper-and-lower-neighbor notes preceding a note of resolution that is consonant with the underlying harmony, as in F4b, sometimes with an inverted-mordent ornamentation (F4c); or (2) an ascending half step to the note of resolution, as in F4f. It often has a short descending prefix up to three notes long (F4d–e). Reinhardt frequently interpolates a single passing note lying outside of the basic diminished-seventh collection, as in the pitch F♮ in F4e. F4g is actually an ascending half-diminished-seventh, rather than a fully diminished, arpeggiation but is here grouped with the other examples for convenience.

F5: An ascending arpeggiated triad with a prefix consisting of a turn (F5a) or a lower-neighbor note (F5b and F5c).

F6: An ascending arpeggiated triad followed by a lower-neighbor note (with an inverted mordent) to the arpeggiation's final, apex pitch.

Formulas 7–11 also all involve arpeggiations of some sort.

F7: A descending zigzagging arpeggio. Reinhardt frequently arpeggiates the pitches of a minor triad over its relative major harmony, suggesting an added-sixth major sonority with the fifth omitted, as in the given example from "Hangin' Around Boudon" (7/7/37; mx. OLA 1888-1), in which he outlines a G-minor triad over a B♭-major harmony.

F8: An ascending arpeggio, each note of which has an upper-neighbor prefix.

F9: An ascending arpeggio followed by two descending half steps and then a descending arpeggio. The chromatic descent of two half steps is a typical device of Reinhardt's (see F12–13 and F32–33). Here it links two arpeggiations. The latter portion of the formula thus corresponds to F2.

F10: Alternating rising and falling arpeggiations of a single triad or seventh chord. Reinhardt often repeats this pattern several times in succession, creating a treadmill effect of simultaneous melodic motion and harmonic stasis. It may be introduced with a lower-neighbor prefix of the sort previously noted in F5b (compare with F10a).

F11: A chromatic sequence of alternate descending and ascending arpeggiations. As the four given examples show, this device can take many different forms.

Formulas 12 and 13 each involve a descent of two consecutive half steps.

F12: A descent of two half steps preceded by a downward arpeggio (or a descending pentatonic segment). Its rhythmic and harmonic contexts are both highly variable. The first of the three chromatically adjacent tones may appear either on the beat (as in F12a) or off the beat (as in F12c). And while the arpeggio is usually closely related to the underlying harmony (F12c is an exception in which the pitches D–B–G appear over an A7 harmony), the final three-note cell may express many different scale degrees with respect to the chord root. Thus, in F12a the third note of the chromatic cell is the major sixth of C major; in F12b the equivalent note is the ninth of D7; in F12d it is the third of D minor; and in F12e it expresses the seventh of G7. The different examples shown may well be played with similar or identical fingerings even though their harmonic contexts vary.

F13: A descent of two half steps followed by an upward leap of a major or minor seventh (or, less often, a major or minor sixth). The harmonic context is somewhat less variable than F12's. Generally the two disjunct pitches are the seventh and thirteenth of a dominant harmony (as in

F13a) or the ninth and root (as in F13b), although other contexts occasionally occur. (Note that in the second example of F13c, from "Minor Swing" (11/25/37; mx. OLA 1990-1), the inverted mordent of A and B♮ (rather than B♭) means that there are not three adjacent chromatic tones; this figure could, strictly speaking, be excluded from the present category on the grounds of dissimilarity to the rest, but it has been included for convenience rather than adding a new category.) F13 is almost always preceded by some sort of descending melodic contour such as those seen in F12. Clearly F12 and F13 are closely related, but they are treated independently here because of the distinctiveness of F13's ascending leap.

F14: An ascending major seventh (or, less commonly, an octave) with a lower-neighbor prefix. The prefix, which is generally a half step beneath the second note, usually appears on an even-numbered eighth note within the measure. The harmonic context varies, although the configuration in F14a (from "Festival Swing" [12/26/40; mx. OSW 173-1])—with the ascending leap occurring between the seventh and thirteenth of a dominant-seventh harmony—is common. The ascending leap is always followed by a descent, usually an arpeggiation or pentatonic formation (as in F2 and F3).

The remaining variable formulas, F15–19 are miscellaneous devices that are not readily grouped for purposes of classification.

F15: A "turn" figure. Reinhardt used a range of upper- and lower-neighbor-note devices, often at the beginning of a phrase.

F16: An ascending scalar trichord followed by an inverted mordent and then a descending scalar trichord.

F17: An ascending minor third followed by a whole-step descent, a half step back to the initial pitch, and then a descending scale. This device entered Reinhardt's playing during the mid- to late 1940s, probably in connection with his interest in bebop.

F18: An ascending root-position arpeggio with a passing note interpolated between the arpeggiated chord's root and third. This formula generally begins on the beat, and it appears in both minor (F18a) and major (F18b) variants.

F19: An alternation between a note of constant pitch and (often double iterations of) a lower note that oscillates between two pitches a half step apart. This formula often features a dactylic rhythm. Being fairly repetitive, it sometimes plays the role of a background to surrounding melodic material in the manner discussed in chapter 2.

These, then, are the basic repertory of variable formulas that Reinhardt used in his improvised solos. (As noted, the "context-specific" formulas yet to be discussed are a secondary type of variable formula.)

◎ STABLE FORMULAS ◎

Formulas 20–31, which are comparatively invariant and often derive from specifically guitaristic instrumental techniques, are labeled "stable." The first five, F20–F24, all involve short melodic patterns that are reiterated several times.

F20: Repeated eighth notes of a single pitch with every third note accented. This effect is usually created by alternating groups of three notes played on an open string and three fretted at the same pitch on the adjacent lower string, in which case it sounds at one of the open-string pitches E, B, G, D, or A). Like F19, it can function as a background figure. Though not classified as such here, F20 is somewhat context specific and often occurs near the top of a chorus.

F21: A rising and falling arpeggiation of a major triad with an added sixth (alternatively labeled a minor-seventh chord), with each of the arpeggiation's notes prefixed by an accented half-step lower-neighbor note (on the beat). In the given example, from "Appel Indirect" (6/14/38; mx. 4213-HPP), this figure happens to be the principal motive of a composed theme, but it probably originated as a formula because Reinhardt also plays it in other improvisations, including some that predate "Appel Indirect," suggesting that the other occurrences are not simply thematic quotations.

F22: A repeated set of three ascending eighth notes, the first two of constant pitch and the third oscillating by half step between two or three chromatically adjacent pitches. The lowest note is played on an open string; the middle note, usually a perfect fourth higher, is fretted on the adjacent lower string; and the highest (changing) note is fretted on the same string as the initial note but pitched at or near the fret lying an octave above the open string. Reinhardt usually plays this physically convenient and conceptually undemanding formula at fast tempi.

F23: A rising and falling four-note diatonic scale segment. This formula is generally played in triplets either in continual motion (F23b) or with a quarter note on each boundary pitch interpolated between each set of triplets (F23a). F23a is a component of the figure that Hodeir identified as "accompanimental" in Reinhardt's 1939 solo on "Solid Old Man" (see example 2.1).

F24: A repeated set of four eighth notes with upper- and lower-neighbor notes ornamenting a consonant pitch. This formula usually occurs in the guitar's upper register.

F25–31, the remainder of the stable formulas, are less repetitive than those just described but are still mainly associated with instrumental techniques specific to the guitar.

F25: A tremolo across open strings with simultaneous sounding of the same pitches (unisons), or the pitches a half step lower, fretted on the adjacent (lower) string. Reinhardt used tremolos more often than most other jazz guitarists with the exception of his gypsy jazz imitators.

F26: A semitonal oscillation between a minor triad in first inversion, consonant with the underlying harmony, and its lower neighbor, the latter occurring on the beat. This device is fingered by barring across (stopping at the same fret) the instrument's highest three strings.

F27: First-inversion diminished triads ascending by minor thirds. F27 most often occurs with arpeggiations of the triads (as in F27a) and sometimes involves tremolo effects. It is fingered by stopping the G and high-E strings at the same fret with the second and third fingers, and the intervening B string one fret lower with the first finger. Strict transposition then requires only sliding this finger arrangement up the fingerboard three frets at a time.

F28: An ascending half-step motion replicated at successive downward octave transpositions, with audible glissando-like finger slides.

F29: A chromatic descent in which single notes alternate with dyads a minor tenth and minor seventh above them (the latter pair of notes sometimes sounded simultaneously, sometimes separately).

F30: An ascending arpeggiation of an A7 harmony (usually with added ninth). F30 always includes the guitar's open A string, and it sometimes begins with the open low-E string and fretted G preceding the figure from "Sweet Georgia Brown" (1/31/38; mx. DTB 3524) shown here. This formula also makes use of the open G, B, and high-E strings in the course of the arpeggiation.

F31: A series of chromatically ascending arpeggios above a static open-D-string pedal tone. F31a, from "Confessin' (That I Love You)" (3/35; mx. P 77242), is the more common variant; F31b is a less common version. F31 is mainly associated with the early years of Reinhardt's career. The guitarist uses this formula in the 1937 version of "Sweet Georgia Brown" discussed in chapter 1 (see example 1.6c).

◎ SUPERFORMULAS ◎

Formulas 32–37 are designated "superformulas"—comparatively lengthy patterns, most of which comprise shorter formulas that are fairly invariant (stable).

F32: Two descending melodic half steps, sequentially shifted through three different transposition levels. The paired falling half steps have already been noted in F12–13. In the case of F32, this trichordal cell is played on each of the guitar's three highest strings in turn, usually producing a melodic line whose ambitus is exactly one octave, as in the given example from "Mixture" (4/16/42; mx. 16196). F32 begins to appear in Reinhardt's improvisations from the early 1940s, although he plays a similar figure that transposes two *ascending* half steps through different pitch levels on one of his very first recordings with the Quintet, "Tiger Rag" (12/34; mx. P 77162).[19]

F33: A descent through two half steps as part of a downward melodic sequence with interpolated ascending leaps of a sixth or minor seventh. This formula, which also incorporates the descending chromatic trichord, is more variable than most other superformulas. Its characteristic element is the descending chain of broken sixths, seen here in "Japanese Sandman" (5/17/39; mx. 5081-HPP) between G–E♭ and F–D.

F34: A sequence of ascending arpeggios with a lower-neighbor suffix ornamented by an inverted mordent. The basic melodic pattern, essentially an instance of F6, is repeated successively with alterations to suit the underlying harmonic progression.

F35: A triplet realization of a descending step and arpeggiated triad followed by a descent of two half steps. This superformula, which combines F2 and F12, is very often prefixed by a turn (F15), as in F35a; a short chromatic scale segment, as in F35d; or both, as in F35b. It may continue in various ways, such as with an upward leap, seen in F35c, of the sort already described in F13, or a rising arpeggio as in F35b. It first enters Reinhardt's formulaic vocabulary during the early to mid-1940s.

F36: An ascending arpeggio, each of whose pitches is ornamented by a turn figure. This formula is often heard in Reinhardt's later recordings.

F37: A falling arpeggio with its notes ornamented by turns and connected to one another by a scale segment. F37 is mainly confined to the last four years of Reinhardt's recorded career (from 1949 onward).

◉ CONTEXT-SPECIFIC FORMULAS ◉

The remaining formulas, F38–41, are "context specific": they are strongly associated with specific locations within an improvisation's song form. Fairly flexible in their appearances, they are secondarily classified as variable.

F38: A repeated bent pitch, usually alternating with another note a fairly large interval (normally a perfect fifth) lower. The bent pitch is created by "choking" the string with the left hand (i.e., increasing its tension to produce a pitch higher than the usual one associated with the fret and string being depressed). When the second (lower) pitch occurs in alternation (as in all examples except F38d), it is usually played on the adjacent lower string. Sometimes a third pitch, an octave higher than the lowest one, also alternates with the others, as in F38b from "Ain't Misbehavin'" (4/22/37; mx. OLA 1708-1). The context for this formula is generally the very end or very beginning of a chorus or, less often, of an eight-bar formal section.

F39: A repeated pattern, usually spanning three beats (F39a), consisting of three eighth-note triplets ascending to a single, longer apex pitch. The ascending triplets generally comprise some form of arpeggiated triad, as in F39b. F39 usually occurs toward the end of an eight-bar formal section.

F40: A descending chromatic scale, each of whose pitches is ornamented by a chromatic upper neighbor in the manner of an eighth-note-triplet inverted mordent. The inverted mordent is played by "hammering on" and "pulling off" with the left hand at the fret above the one initially sounded with the plectrum. Like F39, this device is generally associated with the end of an eight-bar formal section.

F41: An arpeggiation, either rising or falling, of a tonic triad followed by a descending arpeggiation of a leading-tone diminished-seventh harmony, ending with a resolution to the tonic note. F41 usually starts on the first beat of a measure so that the final tonic note arrives on the downbeat of the following measure. It almost always begins in the penultimate measure of an eight-bar (or twelve-bar in the case of a blues form) formal unit, acting as a stock cadential device. Reinhardt began using it in the early to mid-1940s.

Brief analyses of six of Reinhardt's solos appear below. Issues of chief concern are (1) how the guitarist's formulas mutually interrelate within his improvisations; (2) how his formulaic usage relates to formal location; and (3) his occasional treatment of formulas as developmental motives. In addition, certain of the solos contain substantial passages devoid of formulas from the given list, and in some of these regions Reinhardt introduces (nonformulaic) motivic development or reuses similar material at equivalent points within different choruses. The interface between formulaic and nonformulaic passages also sometimes involves discontinuities of the sort discussed in chapter 2: melodic paraphrases, background material, and so forth.

Example 3.1 displays an annotated transcription of Reinhardt's version of "After You've Gone." This two-chorus solo contains a single explicit discontinuity, the rifflike interjection bracketed in mm. 3.13–3.16. Formulas are for the most part isolated from one another with little overlap, except in mm. 2.2–2.3, 2.11–2.12, and 5.9–5.12. Reinhardt uses a fairly limited selection of them, of which many appear several times, such as F36, the superformula based on ascending turn figures, which has four occurrences. Compensating for this repetitiveness, Reinhardt plays F36 in several different metric locations: in m. 2.4 it begins on the fourth beat of the bar, in m. 2.21 it begins on beat three, and in mm. 3.5 and 3.21 it starts on beat two.

Reinhardt also duplicates material at equivalent locations in both choruses. Some such material is nonformulaic, like the melodic structure heard in both mm. 2.7–2.9 and mm. 3.7–3.9, whose first appearance introduces F2; its second occurrence simply ends a phrase (m. 3.9), suggesting a truncated version of the first one. Other such replications are formulaic; F6, for example, occurs in m. 2.25 and m. 3.25. In m. 3.25 the guitarist uses this formula, an ascending arpeggio to an inverted mordent (here outlining a D-minor triad) to initiate the superformula F34 in which F6 is reiterated with modifications according to the harmonic context. These repetitions raise a fundamental evaluative issue discussed by Kernfeld in his work on Coltrane.[20] They could be interpreted either as inadvertent symptoms of Reinhardt's flagging inspiration or, more positively, as deliberate unifying strategies that make the second chorus sound like a free variation on the first. Since Reinhardt's intentions are unknown, this aesthetic issue is not definitively resolvable.

⊚ "DJANGO'S TIGER" ⊚
(1/31/46; mx. OEF 26-1)

Whereas "After You've Gone" contains several passages devoid of identified formulas, "Django's Tiger" consists mainly of chains of formulas that transition seamlessly from one to the next, in some cases producing continuous phrases of considerable length. (Both solos are played at a fairly brisk tempo of over two hundred quarter notes per minute.)

EXAMPLE 3.1. Improvisation on "After You've Gone" (1–2/49; mx. CW 49)

EXAMPLE 3.1. *(cont.)*

EXAMPLE 3.1. *(cont.)*

Example 3.2 displays a transcription of Reinhardt's solo and also the final chorus, in which he "trades fours" with Stéphane Grappelli. The theme's harmonies are based on the second strain of the Original Dixieland Jazz Band's classic "Tiger Rag."

Reinhardt's main solo occurs during the first two full choruses. Example 3.2 suggests that quite sharp distinctions exist between (1) passages involving little or no formulaic material such as mm. 1.1–1.7, 1.29–1.31, 2.5–2.8, and 2.15–2.16, (2) passages containing a large number of variable formulas such as mm. 1.9–1.28 and 2.20–2.31, and (3) sections

EXAMPLE 3.2. Improvisation on "Django's Tiger" (1/31/46; mx. OEF 26-1)

EXAMPLE 3.2. *(cont.)*

Example 3.2. *(cont.)*

EXAMPLE 3.2. *(cont.)*

EXAMPLE 3.2. *(cont.)*

Example 3.2. *(cont.)*

of accompaniment-like "background" material such as the (bracketed) repetitive ostinato in mm. 1.32–2.4 or the send-off-like chordal interjections in mm. 2.17–2.19. ("Django's Tiger" has no composed melody that could be paraphrased.) This parsing invites a performer-oriented interpretation such as was proposed for "Liza" in chapter 2 (example 2.16). The nonformulaic material, which appears to have been conceived essentially spontaneously, may stem from a comparatively high creative level (a high frequency of cognitive event cycles in Sarath's terms). Likewise, the formulaic passages would demand slightly less of Reinhardt's attentive capacity, because they utilize material that is already familiar to him, and the background passages allow him a moment to gather inspiration for future musical events. If so, it may not be coincidental that one of the nonformulaic foreground passages, mm. 2.5–2.8, is immediately preceded by the repetitive background pattern at the start of the second chorus, and another appears at the very beginning of the performance, since in both instances Reinhardt has had a brief opportunity to mentally prepare the new, foreground material.

In the several heavily formulaic regions of "Django's Tiger," Reinhardt links the formulas together in a variety of ways. Mm. 1.18–1.29 contain a continuous eleven-bar musical phrase consisting almost exclusively of eighth notes, nearly every one of which is formulaic in origin. Often the guitarist pivots seamlessly between two formulas by means of melodic features common to both. On the upbeat to m. 1.21, for instance, he plays F15, the turn figure that here ornaments the pitch C♯, which is consonant with the underlying A-major harmony. The first four eighth notes in m. 1.21, B♯–C♯–F♯–E, might imply that Reinhardt is initiating the superformula F36 (an ascending arpeggiation of a triad with each pitch ornamented by a turn). However, in the second half of that bar he instead plays a pair of descending half steps, C♯–C–B, a pattern found in several different formulas. This suggests F12 during the middle of m. 1.21 (F♯–E–C♯–C–B), but the two descending half steps immediately dovetail with the beginning of the superformula F32, in which this three-note cell is reiterated at various transpositions. Reinhardt uses a similar technique two measures later, where the two descending half steps act as a pivot between F12, in m. 1.23, and F4, the ascending arpeggiation of a diminished harmony, in the next bar. All told, "Django's Tiger" demonstrates that the key to improvisational fluency lies not in the formulas' singular characteristics but in the melodic similarities that enable them to be linked together sequentially.

◎ "SOLITUDE" ◎
(4/21/37; mx. OLA 1706-1)

The final eight bars of Reinhardt's solo on "Solitude" were discussed in the previous chapter with regard to the guitarist's use of a structural marker (see example 2.7). The solo as a whole contains several explicit paraphrases of Duke Ellington's melody, which is shown above the transcription in example 3.3, as well as formulaic passages and apparently spontaneously conceived material. (The melodic paraphrases and concluding structural marker are bracketed in the transcription.) The first and last eight-bar A sections of this thirty-two-bar AABA form both contain paraphrases of the preexisting melody around the beginning of each four-bar section (mm. 1.32–2.2 and 2.5–2.7; mm. 2.24–2.25 and 2.29–2.31), and another brief, durationally compressed paraphrase appears at the beginning of the second A section (m. 2.9).

Other regions of the improvisation stray far from Ellington's

EXAMPLE 3.3. Improvisation on "Solitude" (4/21/37; mx. OLA 1706-1)

EXAMPLE 3.3. *(cont.)*

EXAMPLE 3.3. *(cont.)*

melody. Aside from the melodic paraphrases, formulas account for most of the first sixteen bars, though their frequency decreases as Reinhardt approaches the bridge (mm. 2.17–2.24), which contains just one formula, F4 (m. 2.17). Through this point, the improvisation charts a course from the general to the specific: the original melody is, presumably, common to most other renditions of this theme; formulaic material is associated with Reinhardt's oeuvre as a whole; and nonformulaic, spontaneous passages are specific to this particular solo. In the last eight measures Reinhardt returns to both the original melody and his formulaic vocabulary. The appearance of the stable formula, F25, in mm. 2.27–2.28 is an example of physical instrumental considerations superseding conceptual (in this case harmonic) matters because this formula's tremolo across the guitar's highest open strings, E–B–G–D, bears scant relationship with the secondary dominant D7 harmony underlying these measures. Nonetheless, F25 transitions seamlessly into the succeeding dyadic tremolos that, in m. 2.29, subtly begin to recall the original melody as the pitches A and G enter in the upper voice.

In mm. 2.10–2.11 Reinhardt plays a rising and falling arpeggiation of a C-major, and then a D-major, harmony, with each consonant pitch ornamented by a half-step lower-neighbor prefix. This figure, labeled F21*, is similar but not identical to F21 as it appears in figure 4.1 (where it embellishes an added-sixth harmony rather than a triad). The two consecutive iterations of this melodic pattern, transposed according to the harmonic context, indicate that Reinhardt's formulas are not simply variable entities that can take many forms; they can also undergo developmental processes within a given solo.

◉ "FESTIVAL SWING" ◉
(12/26/40; mx. OSW 173-1)

Reinhardt's twenty-four-bar solo on the blues "Festival Swing" (example 3.4) alternates between formulaic material and passages of motivic development. The first half of each twelve-bar chorus (mm. 11.1–11.6 and 12.1–12.5) is mainly formulaic; indeed, the opening of the first chorus is virtually saturated with formulas. Reinhardt begins with the stable formula F20—alternating groups of three notes between the open G string and the same pitch fretted on the D string—which frequently appears around the beginning of a chorus, as it does here. The second half of the first chorus (mm. 11.7–11.12) is largely devoted to a repeated turn-like figure (F–E♭–D–E♭). While this figure can be labeled an instance of F15, its multiple consecutive reiterations and lack of any prefixlike function, as is the norm with F15, are atypical and draw special attention to it. Reinhardt develops the turn figure motivically over the course of these measures (in the second half of m. 11.8 through m. 11.9 the final E♭ is omitted, with D and then G substituted instead, and at the end of m. 11.10, F–E♭–D forms a descending prefix to a new, longer phrase). At the solo's close (mm. 12.10–12.12) he refers back to the first chorus by reintroducing this same figure. (On the recording his final few notes are obscured by the next soloist's entrance.)

"Festival Swing" also illustrates how melodic patterns associated with a given formula can receive very different rhythmic realizations. Compare, for instance, m. 12.5—which opens with F14, the distinctive lower-neighbor half-step prefix to an ascending major seventh followed by a descending line (that includes an instance of F2)—with the equivalent region of the preceding chorus (m. 11.5–11.6). In the first chorus an identical series of pitches (excluding the initial lower-neighbor-note D) appears with an entirely different rhythmic profile (labeled as F14*). Specifically, a rest of two whole beats intervenes between the successive notes E♭ and D (m. 11.5), significantly altering the presentation of the major-seventh interval that is F14's most salient melodic feature (m. 12.5). These contrasting realizations of the same pitch ordering are the sort of procedures that might be overlooked were Reinhardt's formulas too strictly defined.

"Festival Swing" contains a passage in which, like the appearance of F25 toward the end of "Solitude," surface-level melodic material

Example 3.4. Improvisation on "Festival Swing" (12/26/40; mx. OSW 173-1)

bears little direct relationship to the underlying harmonies. In mm. 12.8–12.9 Reinhardt first plays the pitches B and D over the tonic (C-major) harmony followed by an arpeggiation of an F-major triad (F10) over the dominant-seventh (G7) harmony. He thus creates chromaticism through altering a given formula's harmonic context: playing this particular version of F10 over G7 implies a dominant-eleventh chord rather than the straightforward triad it would articulate over an F-major harmony.[21] This sort of harmonic usage will be discussed further in chapter 4.

◉ "COQUETTE" ◉
(1/31/46; mx. OEF 25-1)

In his solo on "Coquette" (example 3.5), Reinhardt relates formulaic passages to separate regions of motivic development by highlighting, in both cases, the same structural operation: close-range octave transposition. During this two-chorus improvisation, formulas most often occur during the second half of each eight-bar section (the theme has a standard thirty-two-bar AABA form). Passages of eighth-note triplets featuring the superformula F35 (and in some cases F32 also) appear in mm. 2.12–2.15, 2.21–2.24, 3.8–3.17 (preceded by another superformula, the ascending ornamented arpeggio F36, which leads into the second A section of Reinhardt's second chorus), and 3.29–3.32. (As noted, "After You've Gone" also features this sort of consistent reuse of certain superformulas.) "Coquette" contains one very brief melodic paraphrase, in m. 2.17, the beginning of the first chorus's bridge (bracketed in the example).

Perhaps this solo's most notable feature, however, originates in its opening bars (mm. 1.32–2.3). Reinhardt starts by playing the dyad G♯–A in the guitar's middle register. He then immediately uses the G♯–A dyad as the melodic kernel of F28, a formula involving successive downward octave transpositions. In this case the dyad descends from the guitar's extreme upper register through two such octave displacements so as to arrive at its original pitch level again. (The transcription is annotated with boxes enclosing the relevant notes and octave transpositions between them labeled "8ve.") Over the course of the solo Reinhardt periodically reuses this same procedure: a dyad comprising either a whole or half step is immediately, or very shortly, transposed down by an octave. After the first occurrence, each subsequent use of this technique is in a non-formulaic context. Reinhardt generally highlights the dyads in question by means of consecutive repetitions or by locating them at the apex of a phrase's melodic contour, and he also often accents them dynamically.

The downward octave-transposition operation is featured in mm. 3.1–3.2, where the dyad C♯–B functions as a major seventh (C♯) "resolving" to the added sixth (B) of the underlying tonic D-major harmony. The same harmonic relationship exists in mm. 3.19–3.20, where an F♯–E dyad represents the major seventh and sixth of a G-major chord. Octave transposition of a neighbor-note dyad recurs in mm. 3.23–3.24, where a four-note melodic fragment containing the pitches D–D–D–C♯ appears at two different octave levels. In the next two bars (mm. 3.25–3.26) Reinhardt reiterates the dyad A–B before transposing it to a lower octave in

EXAMPLE 3.5. Improvisation on "Coquette" (1/31/46; mx. OEF 25-1)

EXAMPLE 3.5. *(cont.)*

117

EXAMPLE 3.5. *(cont.)*

m. 3.28. Another explicit transpositional procedure, based on upward displacements by a perfect-fifth interval, also occurs in this solo. Between m. 2.26 and m. 2.29 a figure consisting of a rising four-note arpeggiation followed by a downward step is twice transposed upward by a perfect fifth (with slight adjustments in order to remain within the key of D major). (The downward steps create whole-step dyads at the figure's apex [that is to say, E–D, B–A, and F♯–E], much like the octave-transposed dyads elsewhere.)

"Coquette" is atypical; Reinhardt does not routinely generate nonformulaic regions of a solo from a formula's underlying formal operation, at least not so explicitly. Nonetheless, this performance reveals that his formulas are not simply ossified melodic building blocks but rather are based on general, adaptable structural principles that they may share either with one another or with nonformulaic passages.

◎ "MONTMARTRE" ◎
(4/5/39; mx. OSW 63-1)

"Montmartre" (example 3.6), which has the alternative title "Django's Jump," is another thirty-two-bar AABA form. Reinhardt's single-chorus solo contains sharp discontinuities during the first four bars of the bridge (mm. 2.17–2.20), where the guitarist plays a send-off-like passage in octaves, and at the end (mm. 2.31–2.32), where he switches to chordal playing as he prepares to accompany the next soloist (cornetist Rex Stewart). The latter device, simultaneously providing closure to the foregoing improvisation and heralding that which follows, functions much like the structural marker at the end of "Solitude" (examples 2.7 and 3.3).

The solo features three different recurring motivic figures, each of them formulaic in origin. First, Reinhardt introduces both halves of the chorus with a repeated pitch—F♭ (enharmonically the high open E string) in m. 1.32 and G in m. 2.16—labeled F20* (the asterisk indicates that this is not this stable formula's typical form since it appears as eighth-note triplets rather than ordinary eighth notes with every third note accented). Second, in mm. 2.7–2.8, F5 (an ascending arpeggio with a half-step lower-neighbor prefix) functions as a basic melodic cell for a series of rising eighth-note arpeggios leading into the second eight-bar formal section (the arpeggios express in turn an F-minor triad, an A♭-major triad, and then another, incomplete, A♭-major triad). Reinhardt restates F5 in the second half of the bridge (m. 2.21), where, clearly treating formulaic material developmentally, he initiates the first of three successive triplet-eighth-note figures (labeled "γ" in example 3.6) that ascend to the pitch B♭; the second and third of these are both based on F4. He reiterates motive γ two final times in mm. 2.26–2.27. The third motivic use of formulas in this solo occurs fleetingly in mm. 2.13–2.14, where F14 appears at two different transpositional levels, producing a short descending melodic sequence.

Reinhardt also creates nonformulaic motivic development with the two melodic figures labeled "α" and "β" in example 3.6. Motive α occurs five times, always at the end of a phrase (mm. 2.1, 2.3, 2.6–2.7, 2.25, and 2.30–2.31). It usually begins with quarter notes on the first two beats of a bar (except for its final statement, which starts on beats three and four of m. 2.30), and its pitches all belong to the tonic A♭-major triad; the first note is generally the motive's apex pitch, the second is the nadir, and the third usually lies in a register between the preceding two. By playing the motive around the beginning and end of both the first and last eight-bar A sections, Reinhardt gives the solo a semblance of large-scale formal symmetry. In addition, at the close of these two A sections (mm. 2.5–2.7 and mm. 2.29–2.31) motive α is preceded by essentially the same melodic figure (which includes F13). The motive labeled β—three

EXAMPLE 3.6. Improvisation on "Montmartre" (4/5/39; mx. OSW 63-1)

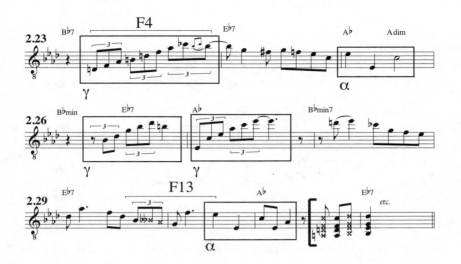

EXAMPLE 3.6. *(cont.)*

eighth-note triplets ascending from B♭ to a quarter-note C (or C♭) a ninth above—is only heard during the first half of the chorus. Its first two appearances immediately follow instances of motive α, while the third (m. 2.10) occurs during the second A section, which is otherwise the solo's most heavily formulaic region.

"Montmartre" illustrates that structural discontinuities and melodic formulas, which have been treated independently in this chapter and the previous one, are both in practice inextricably entwined with other aspects of Reinhardt's musical language such as motivic relationships. Having initially isolated these two especially salient aspects of the guitarist's playing, our next task, in chapter 4, is to recontextualize them so that we might gain a less reductive, more multidimensional understanding of his music.

◦ 4 ◦

THREE
CLASSIC SOLOS

Although this book does not, for the most part, seek to evaluate Reinhardt's music, if pressed I would date his finest recorded achievements to the late 1930s, when he was consistently playing at an extraordinary artistic level. That phase of his career was abruptly truncated by the outbreak of World War II in September 1939 while he was touring England with the Quintet of the Hot Club of France. When hostilities were announced, Reinhardt quickly returned to continental Europe, but Stéphane Grappelli, the Quintet's other soloist, stayed in Britain until 1946. The guitarist managed to sustain a surprisingly active performing career during the war considering his imperiled status as a gypsy under Nazi domination, although he had no opportunities to play with musicians as accomplished as either Grappelli or the Americans he had occasionally worked with during the 1930s.

Soon after the war ended, Reinhardt visited England again and was reunited with Grappelli. The recordings they made for two different record labels, Swing and Decca, on January 31 and February 1 of 1946, with a British rhythm section reviving the original Quintet's all-string instrumentation for the first time in over six years, document the guitarist once again in peak form. Yet the circumstances were fleeting; Grappelli did not immediately return to France, and later that year Reinhardt embarked on an American tour as a guest soloist with the Duke Ellington Orchestra. By then the new jazz style called bebop had burst on the scene, and in the years before he died in 1953 Reinhardt began incorporating some of its innovations into his own music, a gradual process addressed in chapter 5. For both personal and musical reasons, therefore, his playing never again quite reached the level and consistency of the prewar period.

Before turning to Reinhardt's final years, it is worth taking stock of what he had achieved during his classic period. To that end, this chapter analyzes three complete improvisations: one from immediately before World War II, "I'll See You in My Dreams," and two from the reunion sessions of 1946, "Love's Melody" and "Embraceable You."

◉   "I'LL SEE YOU IN MY DREAMS"   ◉

Accompanied only by guitarist Pierre "Baro" Ferret and bassist Emmanuel Soudieux, Reinhardt recorded Isham Jones's "I'll See You in My Dreams" (mx. OPG 1721-1) on June 30, 1939, just weeks before the outbreak of World War II. His solo continually toys with the song's underlying form, sometimes accentuating its periodicity with discontinuities and melodic figures that recur at equivalent locations in separate choruses, and sometimes contravening the hypermeter.

Example 4.1 shows Jones's original melody in the uppermost staff and divides Reinhardt's improvisation between the lower three staves so as to distinguish between material designated as the musical foreground, melodic paraphrases, and background (second, third, and lowest staves, respectively). Melodic formulas are also labeled on the score. The song has a thirty-two-bar form comprised of four eight-bar phrases, ABAC. Each eight-bar phrase contains two four-bar subphrases, and the original melody consists almost entirely of either whole or half notes (or two whole notes tied together). The only points of relative rhythmic variety are the quarter notes in m. 11 and m. 15 of the chorus.

Reinhardt plays a rubato a cappella guitar introduction that opens with a paraphrase of the theme, harmonized in three-part chords, but deviates from the composed melody after its first four notes, when he plays the pitches C and B♭ in the upper voice (mm. 3–4). After the introduction, the rhythm section enters in tempo, and Reinhardt's first chorus consists of a free rendition of the original melody. Alterations to this melody, and interpolations, grow increasingly extensive as the chorus unfolds (interpolations have been assigned to the foreground level, shown on the second staff in example 4.1). The first interpolation (m. 1.3) mirrors that of the introductory passage, with the insertion of the pitches C and B♭ (creating an upward melodic leap to a pitch lying a perfect fourth above the final note of the first four-bar phrase, which is replicated in m. 1.6 by the pitch G♮, likewise not part of the written melody). Reinhardt reuses the B♭–C dyad as a salient motivic feature

EXAMPLE 4.1. Improvisation on "I'll See You in My Dreams" (6/30/39; mx. OPG 1721-1)

Example 4.1. *(cont.)*

EXAMPLE 4.1. *(cont.)*

EXAMPLE 4.1. *(cont.)*

EXAMPLE 4.1. *(cont.)*

EXAMPLE 4.1. *(cont.)*

EXAMPLE 4.1. *(cont.)*

EXAMPLE 4.1. *(cont.)*

Example 4.1. *(cont.)*

EXAMPLE 4.1. *(cont.)*

EXAMPLE 4.1. *(cont.)*

EXAMPLE 4.1. *(cont.)*

later in the solo. These two notes are the boundary pitches of the repeated ascending figure with which he begins his first improvised chorus (mm. 2.1–2.4), and the same pitches, with C acting as an upper neighbor to B♭, lie at the apex of the falling melodic gestures that open the following chorus (mm. 3.1–3.3).

The next interpolation within the thematic exposition occurs at m. 1.8, where Reinhardt introduces the formula F15, a chromatic turn figure around D♮ that will also subsequently recur. As he finishes playing the theme (mm. 1.28–1.32), the guitarist introduces a repetitive background figure based on the context-specific formula F38, here oscillating between the guitar's open D string and the same pitch an octave higher, tritonally bisected by the note A♭; this is his farthest departure yet from the original melody. By suppressing the theme's final phrase, Reinhardt signals that this is not an ending but rather the beginning of a foray into uncharted musical territory; the background passage is what Steve Larson calls a "cadence avoidance," a melodic gesture overriding an underlying point of harmonic closure.[1] In this instance Reinhardt plays the harmonically dissonant tritones in a polyrhythmic melodic pattern involving a reiterated three-beat figure against the duple meter (mm. 1.30–1.32). (The same rhythmic device also appears elsewhere in the solo, usually marking a significant structural downbeat [at the beginning of a four- or eight-bar section] by ceasing the cross-rhythms as they coincide with the underlying hypermeter; it occurs, for instance, at mm. 2.2–2.4, where the three-beat-long motives precede the hypermetrical downbeat at m. 2.5, and also, more briefly, at the equivalent point during the second half of the same chorus at mm. 2.19–2.21.) The guitarist plays another background figure, whose pitches recall the initial one, in the second chorus's final bars (mm. 2.29–2.32). Here he supplements the D–A♭ tritone with the tonic note, F, to create an oscillating arpeggiated diminished triad that intensifies the music's forward impetus, militating against the sense of repose created by the tonic harmony's concurrent arrival. The repetitive figures that conclude each of the first two choruses also allow him a few moments to plan more complex material for the top of each upcoming new chorus.

Another strategy that Reinhardt uses to gather inspiration when nearing a new chorus is to paraphrase the preexisting melody as the preceding chorus draws to a close. In his first solo chorus he follows a three-bar background figure (consisting of repeated eighth-note E♮s) in mm. 2.22–2.24 with an E♭ on the hypermetrical downbeat (m. 2.25), exactly where the same note appears in the original melody. Then, in the next two bars (mm. 2.26–2.27), he plays a durationally condensed melodic paraphrase (the scalar descent, A–G–F–E–D, written mainly in half notes in the original melody, is played in eighth notes) followed by the formula F1 and the background diminished-triad arpeggiation mentioned earlier.

The guitarist plays a lengthier melodic paraphrase as the penultimate chorus concludes (mm. 3.25–3.32). The new chorus's onset is demarcated less emphatically than in the previous two, though, because he plays no background material and furthermore elaborates the paraphrase so as to melodically elide one chorus's ending with the beginning of the next. The passage in question is between mm. 3.30–3.31, where an extended series of quarter-note triplets begins. Figure 4.1 shows mm. 29–32 of the written melody on the uppermost staff, mm. 1–8 on the lowest, and mm. 3.29–4.4 of Reinhardt's solo between them on the mid-

Fɪɢ. 4.1. Dual paraphrase relationships at the end of the penultimate chorus of "I'll See You in My Dreams"

dle staff. The guitarist's first four notes in m. 3.30, D–F–G–A, para-phrase the written melody's final four-bar phrase, which starts a bar ear-lier in the original (he has already paraphrased the theme's first two pitches in m. 3.29); the pitches in question are bracketed and connected by a straight line in figure 4.1. The final quarter-note triplet in m. 3.30 and the first in m. 3.31 (the pitches C and G) are interpolations, not found in the theme, but the next note, F♮, corresponds to the original melody's final tonic note, which is displaced a quarter-note triplet later (again, these pitches are bracketed). Reinhardt's F♮ is anything but a point of arrival, however, since it occurs midphrase. The pitches that fol-low it in m. 3.31, A, C, and D (bracketed beneath the middle staff in fig. 4.1), retrospectively make the immediately preceding paraphrase sound like a reference not to the final written phrase of the chorus that is about to conclude but to the opening phrase of the next one. Since the notes A, C, and D paraphrase the beginning of the original melody's *second* four-bar phrase, they suggest a connection between the foregoing D–F–G–A motive and the theme's first phrase, which contains the same motive. Reinhardt reinforces this connection by playing a G♮ on the downbeat of m. 3.31 since G, rather then F, follows D, F, G, and A at the start of the written theme (again, the Gs are bracketed in the figure).

The written melody's final phrase, paraphrased at the close of the third chorus, was supplanted in the previous two by Reinhardt's cadence-avoidance figures, and the guitarist also withholds it in his last chorus as the performance winds to a close. A very subtle reference to the original theme can nevertheless be heard in the notes D and F during the second half of mm. 4.29 of example 4.1, displayed on the next-to-lowest staff. Indeed, as noted, the guitarist played these same pitches as part of the formula F1 exactly one chorus earlier (m. 3.29) before reiterating them within more extensive paraphrase material. (The same two notes also appeared in the arpeggiated D-diminished triad articulated by the cadence avoidance in mm. 2.29–2.32, although in that case a paraphrase relationship seems too tenuous to assert from an external perspective.)

Reinhardt plays the formula F15, first heard as an ornamentation of the melodic pitch D in m. 1.8, at equivalent points in subsequent choruses; it reappears, transposed an octave higher, at mm. 2.8 and 3.9. He also uses this formula to embellish the note E♭ at the corresponding locations within the second halves of the first and third choruses (mm. 1.24 and 3.24), and, although it does not appear at m. 2.24, nor during either half of the final chorus, the guitarist plays an E♭ on the first beat of the twenty-fifth bar in every chorus. This consistently accentuates the hypermetrical downbeat of the choruses' final eight-bar phrase with a pitch drawn from the original melody, a note that already stands out in the original since it is both a melodic apex and the only chromatic pitch. In the second and fourth choruses, where the E♭ on the downbeat of m. 25 is not prefixed by F15, Reinhardt instead precedes the hypermetrical downbeats (mm. 2.25 and 4.25) with medium-range stepwise melodic descents spanning the tritone from A to E♭, as shown in figure 4.2. (The stemmed pitches in the figure all receive dynamic accents, as well as being close in register.) In figure 4.2a the E♭ on the downbeat of m. 2.25 directly follows the previously noted three-bar background figure consisting of eighth-note reiterations of the pitch E♮, an instance of the formula

FIG. 4.2. Tritone-spanning melodic descents

F20. In figure 4.2b the descent involves a series of three-beat-long motives that, as elsewhere, creates rhythmic tension, here resolving on the downbeat of m. 4.25 along with the melodic descent's arrival on E♭.

Also recurring between choruses is a melodic figure that integrates both paraphrases and formulaic material (see fig. 4.3). The first of its three occurrences is at mm. 2.5–2.8, where the formulas F2 (a descending arpeggio with upper-neighbor prefix) and F10 (successive rising and falling triadic arpeggiations) precede a paraphrase of the original melody's second phrase, whose half notes, A, C, D, and E, are converted into eighth notes (the E♮ is chromatically altered to E♭). F1 follows, here arpeggiating the underlying tonic harmony like the preceding F10. Reinhardt slightly alters this melodic complex in each of its two subsequent occurrences: at m. 3.5 he replaces the initial F2 with a more extensive iteration of F10, and at m. 3.21 he initially duplicates the material at m. 2.5 more closely but omits F1. Even when he repeats the same material verbatim in separate choruses, he varies its metric location; thus the F♮ at the nadir of F10 occurs on the downbeats of mm. 2.6 and 3.6, but a beat later at m. 3.22.

Jazz improvisation has, in recent years, often been theorized as a collective process based on group interaction; ensemble musicians, both soloists and rhythm section players, engage in a social activity in which each continually responds musically to what the others are playing.[2] This aptly captures an important element of jazz performance, particularly in postbebop styles, which tend to be especially dialogic. But Rein-

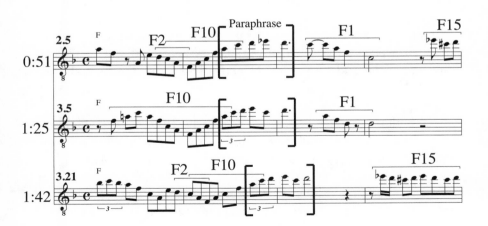

Fig. 4.3. Recurrent material in Reinhardt's solo.

hardt's playing, even though it mostly occurs in a group setting, is a highly individual, solo art. Like many swing era improvisers, the guitarist engages in comparatively little explicit creative interaction with his accompanists, whose markedly subordinate musical roles principally involve sustaining the rhythmic pulse and articulating the harmonic form. Musical interaction is, for Reinhardt, more of a self-directed process. In "I'll See You in My Dreams," he plainly creates a wealth of relationships between his characteristic discontinuities, his habitual formulaic repertory, and the original theme's melody and metric structure. Throughout this inner dialogue between his customary musical practices and preexisting thematic elements, newer material, more spontaneous in conception, also emerges.

In "I'll See You in My Dreams," this more spontaneous material occurs mainly during the first half of each chorus and often involves motives that undergo successive modified repetitions. In mm. 2.1–2.4, for instance, an arpeggiated gesture rising a major ninth from B♭ to C first occurs with an A♮ lower-neighbor prefix; then as two B♭–D–G–C figures, in different metric locations; then with the D♮ chromatically inflected to D♭ (a change dictated by the underlying harmonic shift from B♭ major to B♭ minor in m. 2.3); and finally (m. 2.4) with a B♭ suffix to the apex pitch, C, which leads directly into the first of the recurring melodic complexes shown in figure 4.3 (m. 2.5–2.8). The melodic complex is itself followed by another, more extensive, passage of new material featuring a single motive that is likewise reiterated with continual slight alterations: the chromatically descending sequence of motives based on an ascending minor seventh that dovetails with the first medium-range tritonal descent from A (m. 2.19) to E♭ (m. 2.25) (see fig. 4.2). Other passages featuring modified motivic repetitions are at mm. 3.1–3.4 (where Reinhardt plays a two-bar motive twice in succession); mm. 3.12–3.14 and 3.16–3.20; and mm. 4.6–4.14 and 4.17–4.20 of the final chorus, which both involve arpeggiated motives with the guitar's high A♮ at their apex.

Whether the general design of Reinhardt's 1939 solo was at all preconceived or whether it was invented on the spot is unknowable; the guitarist never recorded another version of "I'll See You in My Dreams" that could be compared with the present one. Still, this single rendition illustrates the many dimensions of prior musical knowledge that he brought to bear on any performance, knowledge that, through a combination of experience and inspiration, he was able to integrate in a seemingly infinite variety of ways.

Reinhardt's version of "Love's Melody" (mx. DR 10026-1), recorded in London on February 1, 1946, encompasses two full choruses at a moderately slow tempo (quarter note = 98). The first chorus consists of Grappelli's free interpretation of the composed melody, and the second is Reinhardt's solo; an annotated transcription is shown in example 4.2. The guitarist's improvisation features formulas that interrelate with procedures of motivic development, as well as material that recurs not between choruses, as in "I'll See You in My Dreams," but rather at equivalent points within different subsections of a single chorus. The solo also provides a good illustration of Reinhardt creating chromaticism by varying the harmonic context of certain recurrent formulas.

He begins his thirty-two-bar solo with an instrumental break—the rhythm section rests—at m. 1.40 and plays another break in the final measure of every eight-bar formal section (mm. 2.8, 2.16, and 2.24). Example 4.2 labels each melodic formula and brackets two instances of musical discontinuity. The first discontinuity is in mm. 2.17–2.19, where Reinhardt plays a background figure whose repetitive melodic profile and lower volume (dynamics have not been indicated in the transcription) contrast with the surrounding passages. This figure mainly consists of a variant of the formula F19, which typically alternates between a static upper pitch and dual iterations of an oscillating lower note rather than both notes moving by half steps as they do here. The other instance of discontinuity, at the end of Reinhardt's solo, is the only clear, though substantially embellished, paraphrase of the original melody.

The solo includes several long-range strategies involving the formulas labeled in example 4.2, some in which formulaic usage progressively changes and others in which formulaic material recurs unaltered. The most prevalent formula is F2, a descending melodic step followed by a triadic arpeggiation; Reinhardt plays it eight times, mainly in conjunction with other formulas in larger melodic motives that gradually evolve over the course of the solo. The motives in question are encircled and labeled "α" and "β" in example 4.2. Within α the formula F2 immediately precedes F1, and in β F2 directly follows F15. Reinhardt plays α mostly in the first half of the solo (mm. 2.7, 2.9, and 2.17) and β mainly during the second half (mm. 2.14, 2.20, 2.22, and 2.25). This gives the solo both continuity (the reiteration of F2) and variety (the alteration of F2's immediate melodic contexts).[3] Indeed, the three appearances of α (F2 followed by F1) are within a region of the solo that contains two additional

EXAMPLE 4.2. Improvisation on "Love's Melody" (2/1/46; mx. DR 10026-1)

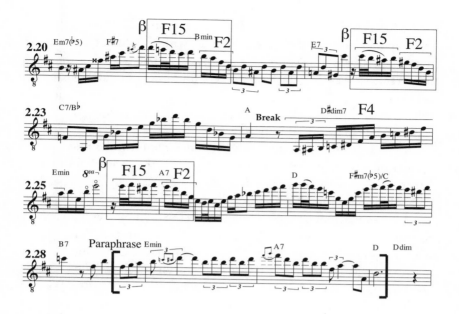

EXAMPLE 4.2. *(cont.)*

reiterations of F1 that are independent of F2, at mm. 2.11 and 2.19, shortly after the background interpolation. (All four occurrences of F1 differ from the formula's more usual form: its rhythmic profile is normative, but its pitches would ordinarily arpeggiate a full descending triad instead of the nontriadic configurations found here.)

Example 4.2 indicates that Reinhardt does not simply subject these formulaic figures to transpositions matching the underlying harmonic changes. The first two instances of α (mm. 2.7 and 2.9), for example, have identical intervallic structures; the second is an exact transposition of the first, a perfect fourth upward. The accompanying harmonies do not share the same transpositional relationship; the first (m. 2.7) is a D-major harmony while the second (m. 2.9) is E minor, a whole-step upward transposition of the chord's root, as well as a shift in quality from major to minor. Consequently, in m. 2.7 the α motive descends from the underlying chord's major seventh through its fifth whereas its transposed form in m. 2.9 descends from the underlying chord's major ninth through its minor seventh. This is typical of Reinhardt's musical language; rather than having fixed harmonic contexts, formulas can be brought into various different relationships with the underlying harmony (probably with the same left-hand fingering each time). The guitarist applies basically the same technique, with one slight modification, to the β motive in mm. 2.20–2.21 and m. 2.22. The second of these is a minor third lower than the first—except for its penultimate note, which is lowered an additional semitone—but the underlying harmonies are related differently; mm. 2.20–2.21 contain a progression from F♯7 to B minor, while in m. 2.23 the chord is E7.

Reinhardt also varies the harmonic context of formulas that recur at approximately equivalent points within each of the chorus's four eight-bar sections, much like his chorus-to-chorus replications in "I'll See You in My Dreams." Figure 4.4 vertically juxtaposes all of his solo's one-bar breaks—at the end of each eight-bar section—along with the three measures that follow each of them. In three of the four breaks Reinhardt plays F4 (the exception is at m. 2.8, where he plays F27), using a different variant each time. In addition, a virtually identical melodic structure containing F2 (a descent through the pitches E–D–B–G–E–D) occurs during the first two measures of every eight-bar section; each instance is encircled in figure 4.4. Its second and third iterations (mm. 2.9 and 2.17) are constituents of the previously discussed α motive, while the fourth (m. 2.26) is part of the motive labeled β.

Since the F2-based melodic cells do not recur at precisely the same points within each eight-bar section, they exhibit the same sort of fluid relationship with the underlying harmony as the other formulas noted earlier. The second and third instances of the cell are supported by an E-minor (and E-minor-seventh) harmony with which their pitches are fully consonant, but the first and fourth instances occur over a dominant (A-major) chord. In the latter cases, the motive's nonharmonic tones D, B, and G are the underlying chord's eleventh, ninth, and minor seventh. The sort of harmonic recontextualization shown in figure 4.4 is thus slightly different from motive α's, in which the melody and concomitant harmony were transposed by different intervals, altering the relationship between them. Here, the harmony changes while the F2-based cell's pitch content stays constant. The motive's relocation to the measure containing an A-major chord is a metric displacement; the improvised melody lags behind the chord changes.

The solo includes several other examples of Reinhardt creating chromaticism by superimposing triadic melodic structures. On the final beat of m. 2.4, he plays an ascending arpeggiation, F♯–A–C♯, over a D-major harmony, implying D major seventh. He then immediately transposes this figure, whose pitches outline an F♯-minor triad, down-

FIG. 4.4. Comparison of the beginning of each eight-bar section in "Love's Melody"

ward by a whole step at the beginning of m. 2.5 so that it conforms to the new underlying harmony in that measure, E minor. A similar process occurs in mm. 2.13–2.14. Most of m. 2.13 consists of an arpeggiated A♯-minor triadic figure, comprised of the pitches A♯, C♯, and E♯, while the accompanying musicians meanwhile play an F♯-major harmony on the first two beats of this bar and D♯ minor in the second half; the three melodic pitches that Reinhardt plays are the third, fifth, and major seventh of F♯ and the fifth, seventh, and ninth of D♯. At the beginning of the next bar the guitarist uses the same melodic transposition as in mm. 2.4–2.5, shifting the triadic melodic pitches a whole step downward to G♯, B, and D♯, which corresponds to the G♯-minor harmony that underlies the beginning of m. 2.14. Elsewhere he uses triadic structures to express chromaticism without this sort of close-range motivic repetition. In m. 2.27, for example, he superimposes C-major triadic arpeggiations over a chord progression from D major to F♯ half-diminished; in the second half of the bar, the melodic pitches hint at a tritone substitution whose resolution is delayed until the third beat of m. 2.28, where C♮ resolves to B, now the underlying harmonic root.

Reinhardt's use of triadic melodies to express chromatic harmony can be further elucidated by means of Leonard B. Meyer's theory of musical style.[4] Meyer's work on Richard Wagner is especially germane, despite its remote stylistic context. Wagner's harmonic idiom and phrase structures, Meyer argues, arise out of the composer's use of musical leitmotifs (distinctive motives or short melodies with specific referential significance in opera story lines). In order to preserve his leitmotifs' recognizable melodic profiles, Wagner frequently subjected them to strict transpositions, and this preference for strict transpositions led the composer to adopt many of his other signature musical devices: melodic sequences involving chromaticism, deceptive cadences to facilitate modulation, and so forth.[5] Reinhardt's harmonic language, too, is partially driven by the use of strict motivic transposition, a simple technique on the guitar that involves simply shifting any given fingering up or down the instrument's fretboard. The guitarist's propensity to use certain formulas in diverse harmonic contexts was first noted in chapter 3, and "Love's Melody" further exemplifies how just a single formula or motive can be used to articulate many different chromatic harmonic structures. At such times melody, harmony, formulas, and instrumental technique are all reciprocally interdependent, with each determining, or derived from, one another.

Reinhardt recorded George Gershwin's "Embraceable You" (mx. OEF 27-1) just a day before "Love's Melody," on January 31, 1946. Example 4.3 shows the original melody in the uppermost staff and distributes the two-chorus guitar solo across the lower three staves—again, foreground, paraphrase, and background. The improvisation contains relatively few explicit discontinuities except that Reinhardt paraphrases the original theme's final phrase toward the ends of both choruses (mm. 2.29–2.31 and 3.29–3.31), just as he did in "I'll See You in My Dreams" and "Love's Melody." He also plays an extended background digression starting just before the top of the second chorus. Several C–D–E♭ scale segments near the opening of Reinhardt's first chorus, and in several other places, have been interpreted as melodic paraphrases. Since these rhythmic diminutions of the melody's familiar ascending gesture are entirely integrated into the surrounding material and not at all highlighted by audible contrasts, this designation rests on the fact that they occur only in approximately the same formal locations as the comparable passages from the published melody.[6]

Ed Sarath's psychological theory of improvisation and Lee Konitz's related notion of conceptual levels, first discussed in chapter 2, shed light on Reinhardt's creative process in this solo. In terms of speculative creative levels, the performance falls into three sections. The first, spanning almost the entire first chorus, through m. 2.30, alternates between fragmentary replications of the original melody and contributions of the guitarist's own that are mainly nonformulaic. In this respect it recalls the opening chorus of "I'll See You in My Dreams," although many of the thematic references are fleeting and the original material is far more extensive than Reinhardt's typical interpolated filigrees. The second section is the ten-bar background passage that begins with an instance of the formula F20 at m. 2.31—the reiterated E♭ eighth notes at the very end of the guitarist's first solo chorus—and then shifts to repeated quarter-note C♮s, with some eighth-note syncopations during the next chorus's opening eight bars. Far less melodically complex than the surrounding music, this passage suggests a lower creative level than that of the preceding section. By devoting less of his attention to this passage as it unfolds, the guitarist is able to focus more on preparing for the comparatively intricate material that predominates for the remainder of his improvisation, a return to a higher creative level.

It is in this third section, and especially between mm. 3.15 and 3.25,

Example 4.3. Improvisation on "Embraceable You" (1/31/46; mx. OEF 27-1)

EXAMPLE 4.3. *(cont.)*

EXAMPLE 4.3. *(cont.)*

EXAMPLE 4.3. *(cont.)*

Example 4.3. *(cont.)*

EXAMPLE 4.3. *(cont.)*

Example 4.3. *(cont.)*

EXAMPLE 4.3. *(cont.)*

that Reinhardt relies most heavily on his musical formulas, which are labeled in example 4.3. During the first chorus, by contrast, the only heavily formulaic passage is the introductory break, where, while the rhythm section rests, he plays a melodic complex comprised of F12, F15, F2, and F12 leading into the downbeat of m. 2.1 (the first half of this pattern is approximately duplicated at mm. 2.3 and 2.21).[7] Mm. 2.31–3.8 of "Embraceable You" therefore differ from the chorus-ending background figures in "I'll See You in My Dreams" in that they are not immediately followed by nonformulaic foreground material. Still, Reinhardt uses the background figuration as a springboard for a lengthy foreground passage from which melodic paraphrases are almost entirely absent until the final bars of the solo.

Reinhardt's second chorus on "Embraceable You" features comparatively long melodic lines in which a limited number of formulas recur in a loosely cyclical order. Figure 4.5 schematizes the order of formulas between mm. 3.15 and 3.25. The guitarist uses just four different formulas during these measures: F14, F2, F13, and F4. Ordinary arrows indicate the most common successions between formulas; broken arrows indicate secondary, alternate pathways. Beginning in the second half of m. 3.14, a three-formula cycle, {F14–F2–F13}, occurs.[8] This, the passage's primary formulaic network, is represented as a clockwise progression in figure 4.5. The cycle starts over in m. 3.17 with F14 and F2, but instead of completing it with F13 Reinhardt breaks the cycle via the alternate pathway from F2 to F4 (mm. 3.17–3.18), indicated with a broken arrow in figure 4.5. F4 turns out to be merely a digression, however, as it is itself followed by F2 (m. 3.19). The original cycle then resumes, {F2–F13–F14–F2–F13} (mm. 3.19–3.22), until m. 3.23 when Reinhardt breaks it again with another digression to F4, which is followed by F2 as before. There are no other formulas during the solo's remaining measures. Since the cycle breaks for a second time not at F2 but rather at F13, its resumption by a return to F2 from F4 (a purely implicative resumption since the cycle ceases for good with F2) is not where it left off but rather one stage prior, an (indirect) backward progression.

Some of the recurring formulas shown in figure 4.5 have variable harmonic contexts. F13, the most consistent harmonically, is always associated with the dominant, B♭. F4 appears over a tonic diminished (E♭-diminished) chord in m. 3.18 and over a V7/IV (E♭7) harmony in m. 3.24. F2 is linked to either a dominant (B♭7) or a pre-dominant (F-minor) har-

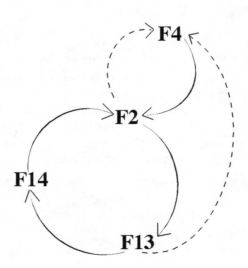

Fɪɢ. 4.5. Formulaic network in "Embraceable You," mm. 3.15–3.25

mony, and F14 is at various times modified to fit a tonic (E♭), dominant (B♭), or pre-dominant (F-minor) chord. So, much as in "Love's Melody," even when Reinhardt uses a considerable amount of formulaic repetition there is great diversity in the melodic formulas' rhythmic realizations, metrical placements, and harmonic settings.

Reinhardt's recordings of early 1946 were made under celebratory circumstances. Along with "Love's Melody" and "Embraceable You," the guitarist and Grappelli performed a swing rendition of "La Marseillaise," retitled "Echoes of France" (1/31/46; mx. OEF 28-1), to honor their nation's recent liberation, as well as the renewal of their artistic collaboration. Perhaps inspired by the occasion, Reinhardt also played several other superlative solos that have been dealt with at some length in these pages. "Liza," discussed in chapter 2, as well as "Django's Tiger" and "Coquette," analyzed in chapter 3, were also recorded over the same two days. Yet in retrospect these discs have an autumnal cast, representing a final capstone on one of jazz's great musical partnerships. In the previous half decade, the world, and the two musicians' lives, had greatly changed. Reinhardt and Grappelli continued to work together sporadically through the late 1940s, but their careers mainly ran separate courses from that time onward. And, although the postwar years saw jazz's popularity fade from its swing era heights, they also saw a wealth of new creative possibilities unleashed by the emergence of bebop. Reinhardt's music would never quite be the same.

◎ 5 ◎

LATE STYLISTIC EVOLUTION

A jazz musician's style, like any other artist's, usually undergoes major changes as he or she reaches creative maturity by absorbing external influences and forging original innovations. Reinhardt is unusual among swing era improvisers, however, in that he never reached a permanent stylistic plateau. Not only did certain of his melodic formulas crystallize only during the second decade of his career, as seen in chapter 3, but he substantially revised his musical language during the late 1940s in response to novel developments that swept the jazz world after World War II. This transformation is the present chapter's focus. Although his playing during the 1930s already had certain characteristics that later gave it an affinity with the new style that became known as bebop, Reinhardt's most immediate response on encountering postwar American innovations was to compose a number of derivative themes, some of them apparently modeled on specific bebop heads. His improvisational language changed more gradually; recordings from the late 1940s document his experimentation with new harmonic and rhythmic resources. While he never shed certain core elements of his earlier style, he had greatly altered his playing by the early 1950s and he was still evolving artistically when he died in 1953.

Reinhardt's career has three stylistic periods.[1] The earliest phase, in which he played the banjo-guitar in the musette style, is clearly delineated from the second in terms of surviving evidence because he made no recordings from late 1928 until mid-1931 while he was recovering after the caravan fire. The second phase, during which he focused exclusively on the six-stringed acoustic guitar, dates from the early 1930s, when he resumed performing. Most of his recordings from these years are with the all-string Quintet of the Hot Club of France, featuring its standard jazz repertory of popular American songs along with original compositions; he also played and recorded sporadically with various other ensembles, some of which included expatriate or touring American musicians. Due to the upheavals of World War II, Reinhardt made comparatively few recordings during the early 1940s, but his final evolutionary phase spanned more than a decade and was quite thoroughly documented after 1946. Again it occurred in tandem with his adoption of a new instrument, the electric guitar. The electric instrument had musical implications in itself; it has a distinctive sonority, potentially much louder volume (making it better suited to larger ensemble contexts), an ability to sustain notes for longer durations, and it enables greater speed because it requires less physical effort to depress its strings.

Reinhardt's playing evolved in response to two principal external influences. First, he drew closer to American swing era jazz conventions by performing alongside horn soloists with a rhythm section of piano, bass, and drums. This was a significant departure from the all-string Quintet, which favored a chugging two-beat rhythmic accompaniment rather than the four-to-the-bar approach typical of contemporary American rhythm sections. The second, and ultimately more transformative, external influence was bebop. Reinhardt's enthusiasm for the new style is especially noteworthy because many established swing era players had little musical interest in it, and some even denigrated it publicly.

Bebop emerged during the early 1940s in competitive after-hours jam sessions, held in upper Manhattan nightclubs, where young musicians—including the drummers Kenny Clarke and Max Roach, pianists Thelonious Monk and Bud Powell, and most notably trumpeter Dizzy Gillespie and alto saxophonist Charlie Parker—devised a musical style that posed significant technical challenges to many older, swing-oriented players. The new idiom was more complex in several respects: it involved greater harmonic chromaticism (especially through the use of substitute harmonies), irregular rhythms (more syncopation and asymmetric phrase lengths), and was often played at extremely fast tempi. It did not spring out of nowhere, however. Parker, during his early career, was heavily influenced by the tenor saxophonist Lester Young, whose solos emphasizing linear melodic development, rather than strictly observing an underlying harmonic structure, presaged bebop's harmonic chromaticism. And another swing era tenor saxophonist, Coleman Hawkins, became probably the greatest single influence on the new style during its formative stages, as the musicologist Scott DeVeaux has detailed. Foremost among Hawkins's musical innovations was what De-Veaux describes as the saxophonist's "ongoing exploration of harmonic improvisation."[2] More overtly than most other swing era soloists, Hawkins emphasized "the practice of deriving notes for an improvised line from the underlying chord progression," often by means of dense, florid melodic activity.[3] During the 1930s Hawkins also incorporated increasing levels of chromaticism into his improvisations, and he pioneered the use of harmonic substitutions in jazz, including the device now known as "tritone substitution."[4] He honed many of these techniques during an extended stay in Europe from 1934 to 1939, most of it spent in France.[5] Hawkins recorded with Reinhardt several times during these years, and the two musicians performed publicly together in Paris, as well as participating in several jam sessions in Amsterdam.[6] Consequently the guitarist had more immediate contact with Hawkins during the period when the saxophonist was formulating his innovations than did jazz musicians based in America.

After 1945 Charlie Parker soon emerged as the single most influential bebop musician, and he remains the style's quintessential exponent. Parker's improvisations, based on the formulaic process that Thomas Owens has documented, feature considerable chromaticism and harmonic substitutions, as well as frequent, elaborate flurries of sixteenth- and thirty-second notes. Parker's phrases also often articulated medium-range melodic structures involving stepwise descents; Owens writes that these "scalar descents . . . are among the most striking elements in [Parker's] musical vocabulary. Further, this scalar organization is a device that he brought into jazz, for his predecessors' music does not contain it."[7] Sometimes Parker based his solos on a linear, less strictly harmonically oriented approach, perhaps a vestige of Lester Young's influence. This process often produced chromaticism not through harmonic substitution but rather by metrically displacing melodic material (often formulaic in origin) against the underlying chord changes. Parker's music was also deeply rooted in the blues, often featuring melodic figures based on the blues scale (primarily the pentatonic minor scale) in a variety of harmonic contexts. Again, this technique suggests more of a linear, scale-driven conception than a strictly chordal one.

Certain bebop-oriented aspects of Reinhardt's late style do not simply originate with the American musicians who influenced him in the 1940s; they were already features of the guitarist's playing during the 1930s. This may partially explain why he was uncommonly receptive to new influences at an advanced stage of his career. Such features include an emphasis on harmonic improvisation and a frequent use of chromaticism, generally by way of passing chords or linearly oriented melodic strategies and displacements (as seen in "Love's Melody") rather than substitutions. His solos from the 1930s occasionally even articulate medium-range scalar descents, like Parker's solos of the following decade.

Reinhardt's 1937 solo on "Paramount Stomp" (12/7/37; mx. OLA 1995-1) exemplifies both a markedly harmonic approach to improvisation and the use of medium-range scalar descents. Example 5.1 contains three staves. The uppermost staff transcribes the melody as played by violinist Grappelli during the recording's first chorus (the nearest thing to an explicit rendition of the original theme), the middle staff consists of Reinhardt's two-chorus solo, and the lowest staff uses Schenkerian analytic notation to interpret the prolongational voiceleading structure implied by Reinhardt's improvisation.[8] (The analytic graph is a free, rather than strictly orthodox, adaptation of Schenkerian notation.) Reinhardt's harmonically oriented approach involves many chordal arpeggiations, graphically denoted by slurs. Aspects of both localized succession and medium-range melodic relationships are graphed in some detail, but only a few selected features will be discussed here. "Paramount Stomp" contains three fairly clear instances of discontinuity, which are bracketed in the lowermost staff: a brief reference to the original melody that opens the solo, a send-off-like chordal passage at the solo's midpoint (mm. 2.15–2.17), and a brief background passage—an ostinato oscillating between the pitches D and F—at mm. 2.25–2.27. The send-off chords participate in the voiceleading of the surrounding measures (specifically with the passage that follows), but the other bracketed regions have no such direct voiceleading relationship with the rest of the solo, an additional reason for regarding them as conceptually separate.

Figure 5.1 indicates that "Paramount Stomp's" harmonic structure consists of the progression IV–I–V7–I repeated four times, with each chord lasting for two bars. (There are also some passing harmonies such as the diminished-seventh chord between IV and I.) The figure also shows the improvisation's background voiceleading structure. The first half of the chorus suggests a sort of modified Schenkerian interruption form: an upper-voice descent from scale degree 6 through scale degree 3 (rather than the typical 2) over the first eight bars, followed by a reassertion of scale degree 6 and a second descent to scale degree 1 at the solo's midpoint. The second half contains a single uninterrupted descent from

Example 5.1. Improvisation on "Paramount Stomp" (12/7/37; mx. OLA 1995-1). Melody as performed by Grappelli, guitar solo, and voiceleading graph

Example 5.1. (cont.)

Example 5.1. *(cont.)*

scale degree ♭6, a chromatic substitute for ♮6 arising from Reinhardt's use of the flattened third of the subdominant, B♭-major harmony in m. 2.17.[9] This solo illustrates that on at least some occasions during the 1930s Reinhardt improvised medium-range melodic descents in the manner that has more often been associated with Parker's bebop era playing. Although these descents do not appear in a majority of Reinhardt's swing era solos, neither is "Paramount Stomp" unique in this respect, as some of the following examples will show.

A 1939 improvisation on "Swing '39" (3/21/39; mx. 4969-1/2HPP), transcribed in example 5.2, contains several chromatic harmonic usages. The formula F11, a sequence of chromatically descending or ascending arpeggiations, occurs in mm. 2.14–2.16, where Reinhardt arpeggiates in turn D-major, E♭-major, D7, and G-minor chords, all superimposed above an underlying D7 harmony. Elsewhere in the same solo, Reinhardt produces chromaticism through metric displacement by anticipat-

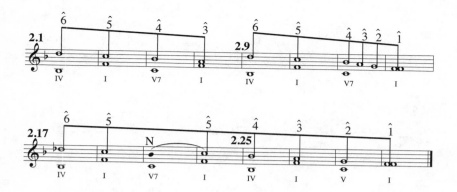

FIG. 5.1. Background melodic structure of "Paramount Stomp"

ing or lagging slightly behind the chord changes. In the second half of m. 2.16, for example, he articulates G minor, anticipating that harmony's arrival in m. 2.17 of the underlying chord structure. Another displacement occurs as he quotes the song "Dinah" in mm. 2.3 and 2.7; over a C7 harmony, he emphasizes the pitches F and D, upper and lower neighbors to the succeeding consonant E♭, in effect delaying the resolution of these notes, which are consonant with the G-minor harmony heard in the previous bars (mm. 2.2 and 2.6). In mm. 2.41–2.44 nonchord tones arise from linear procedures of motivic repetition. Here Reinhardt plays a phrase containing only the pitches B♭, D♭, E♭, and F (a B♭-minor pentatonic subset). The phrase's first two bars occur over a G-minor harmony, with the notes B♭ and F representing the chord's third and seventh, but Reinhardt continues to play the same four notes over the succeeding C7 harmony, now suggesting a superimposed B♭-minor chord. In this instance chromatic dissonance evidently results from the guitarist's focus on linear continuity rather than on strictly observing the chord changes.

Example 5.3, a transcription from Reinhardt's 1936 solo on "Nagasaki" (10/15/36; mx. OLA 1290-1), shows another chromatic effect involving a melody that veers away from the underlying harmonies. While the chord changes mainly alternate between the tonic and dominant of G major, the solo centers on a motive consisting of an eighth-note-triplet inverted mordent followed by a quarter note (amid a lot of other melodic activity this motive is highlighted through varied repetitions). At times Reinhardt's improvised melody has little direct relationship to the predefined chords except toward the end of each eight-bar

Example 5.2. Improvisation on "Swing '39" (3/21/39; mx. 4969-1/2HPP).
Chromaticism in a swing era improvisation

EXAMPLE 5.2. *(cont.)*

EXAMPLE 5.3. Improvisation on "Nagasaki" (10/15/36; mx. OLA 1290-1). Chromaticism in a swing era improvisation

section (as in the arrival on the tonic in m. 3.8 and the passage from mm. 3.13 to 3.16). The guiding musical strategy is rhythmic, with the primary motive undergoing various metric displacements and the most striking dissonances occurring in mm. 3.8–3.10, where the pitches E♭, D♭ (or C♯), E, B, and C occur over a G-major and a D7 harmony.

Example 5.4, also from "Nagasaki," uses Schenkerian notation to illustrate Reinhardt's use of chromaticism in conjunction with a medium-range scalar melodic structure. The solo's first eight bars articulate an ascending linear progression spanning a minor-seventh interval from pitch A (m. 1.2) through G (m. 1.8), indicated with a beam in the voice-leading graph. (Note that, in my reading, a register transfer to a lower octave occurs in m. 1.6 such that the progression culminates a whole step lower, rather than a minor seventh higher, than it began. Thus, in terms of medium-range voiceleading, the consonant pitches C and D, in mm. 1.6 and 1.7, respectively, have less structural weight than the equivalent

EXAMPLE 5.4. Improvisation on "Nagasaki." Medium-range ascent and descent

upper-register pitches—that is, the stemmed A, B, C♯, and D—in the preceding measures.) The chorus's second eight-bar section contains a scalar descent from D♮ to G♮, also involving a registral displacement (m. 1.13). In example 5.4, dissonances generally arise through surface-level semitonal melodic motion (as in mm. 1.9–1.12). In m. 1.4, however, Reinhardt superimposes an incomplete arpeggiated C♯-diminished-seventh chord over the underlying D7. This harmony, functioning as a common-tone diminished seventh that resolves to the tonic G-major chord, appears in conjunction with the upper-register melodic pitch C♯, the raised-fourth scale degree, which better facilitates the ongoing medium-range ascent than would the normative diatonic C♮, whose harmonic tendency is to resolve downward.

Reinhardt's use, during the 1930s, of non-paraphrase-based harmonic improvisation, considerable chromaticism, and medium-range linear voiceleading strategies predisposed him musically toward bebop when he encountered it in the 1940s. The remainder of this chapter first addresses the influence of bebop on Reinhardt's compositions (a body of work that is not otherwise covered in this book) and then explores stylistic changes that occurred in his improvisations during the same period.

The most unequivocal sign of Reinhardt's growing interest in bebop is that some of the themes he composed after World War II were apparently modeled on existing pieces by musicians such as Parker and Gillespie. Reinhardt recorded several of his bebop-influenced compositions in May 1947 on some of the first discs to feature him playing the electric guitar. His theme "Babik (Bi-Bop)" (5/21/47; mx. Fo 1785-R), named for his young son as well as the new style, draws directly on contemporaneous American bebop melodies. Its chord changes are borrowed from George Gershwin's "I Got Rhythm," the most popular basis for bebop contrafacts, and its bridge features a three-note "Salt Peanuts" motive (the signature motive in Gillespie's composition of that name) that follows the underlying cycle-of-fifths progression in much the same way as does the bridge of Charlie Parker's "Red Cross" (1944), which Reinhardt may well have heard. The theme's bridge also highlights the characteristic bebop interval of a tritone between the first and third pitches of each "Salt Peanuts" motive.

Several other derivative pieces appear among Reinhardt's later compositions. His 1951 theme "Impromptu" (5/11/51; mx. P853), which, at approximately quarter note = 360, has one of the fastest tempi of any Reinhardt recording, strongly resembles Gillespie's tune "Bebop," which was also customarily played at breakneck tempo. The second half of "Impromptu's" eight-bar A section resembles the introduction to "Bebop," and the two compositions also have similar bridges that cycle through descending-fifths harmonic progressions (each elaborates the progression with pre-dominant harmonies or tritone substitutions). Both bridges' melodies contain two four-bar phrases in which, as usual with descending-fifths sequences, the second is a whole-step downward transposition of the first (in both cases the two phrases end slightly differently). And in each tune these four-bar phrases contain an initial ascending melodic leap followed by a descending line. "Impromptu" and "Babik (Bi-Bop)," which are probably among Reinhardt's least original compositions, illustrate that in his mid-thirties, rather than being content to simply hone the musical style he had forged during the swing era, he was actively seeking to keep abreast of newer trends. A decade or more after reaching creative maturity, Reinhardt appears to have assimilated elements of bebop in the same way that any novice musician learns to play in a particular style, passing through an imitative phase as he initially grappled with its conventions. This process was reflected in his improvisations as well as his compositions. His recorded solos from the late 1940s onward chart his transition from an experimental stage through an eventual mastery of various bebop techniques.

One of the most straightforward signs of Reinhardt's interest in bebop improvisation is his greater inclination to play double-time passages (usually notated as sixteenth notes) at fairly brisk tempi (previously he tended to do so mainly at medium-to-slow tempi). For instance, in example 5.5, transcribed from his 1948 performance of "Bricktop" (3/10/48; mx. OSW 504-1), he plays the superformula F36 in double time at a tempo of quarter note = 196 (mm. 2.25–2.26). Given the relatively quick tempo, his use of a fixed superformula here probably reflects the fact that rapid passages are easier to execute if they are previously known rather than more spontaneously conceived. (He also plays F36, in double time at a medium tempo, in his 1946 improvisation on "Coquette," as seen in example 3.5.)

The change in Reinhardt's music involved far more substantive transformations of his melodic and harmonic language, however. At first, his playing evolved by means of "mechanical miming," a concept that Meyer describes in his theory of musical style, which was briefly mentioned in the previous chapter. Meyer defines musical style as a "patterning . . . that results from a series of choices made within some set of constraints."[10] Whether they are obeyed or evaded, these constraints

EXAMPLE 5.5. Improvisation on "Bricktop" (3/10/48; mx. OSW 504-1)

EXAMPLE 5.5. *(cont.)*

(i.e., stylistic norms) govern the internal structural syntax of each piece of music. Although bebop did not abandon all aspects of the swing style, it involved certain new constraints to which Reinhardt gradually adapted his playing. Meyer uses the term *mechanical miming* to describe an individual musician who, in trying to imitate an unfamiliar style, reproduces the style's external features without having fully grasped its underlying constraints. True replication, rather than miming, Meyer argues, occurs only when these constraints have been properly understood.[11] (To illustrate, he gives the example of a chess game. In order to play chess a person needs to understand its rules. Although two people can simulate a coherent chess game by simply following detailed instructions about when and how to move the pieces around a board, they are not really "playing chess" unless they comprehend the game's underlying rules.) Mechanical miming and replication may even be indistinguishable from an external standpoint because the distinction between them relates to the artist's intention.

Reinhardt's intentions cannot be known with certainty, of course, but his recordings suggest that he first adopted elements of bebop in a fairly superficial manner—by mechanical miming. He incorporated increasing degrees of chromaticism into his playing in an idiosyncratic fashion, indicating that he had an incomplete understanding of bebop's new conventions. Among the first readily apparent changes in his improvisations was his increased tendency to play conspicuous, unresolved, nonharmonic tones, often at the ends of phrases. (Both swing and bebop improvisers usually end phrases with notes that are either consonant with the underlying harmony or only moderate dissonances such as sevenths or ninths.)[12] He also began occasionally playing arpeggiations that outlined unusual harmonic substitutions or superimpositions with no self-evident consistency akin to the established bebop norm of tritone substitution.

A prominent unresolved dissonance, suggesting a sort of "intentional wrong note," appears in Reinhardt's improvisation on "Bricktop," shown in example 5.5. On the downbeat of m. 3.12 the guitarist ends a phrase with the pitch A♭ over an underlying G-major harmony. The absence of an immediate note of resolution is in marked contrast to the situation eight bars earlier (m. 3.4), where he resolves the same pitch stepwise to G♮, the local chord root and global tonic. Other chromatic techniques in this solo include the minor pentatonic blues-oriented material in mm. 2.1–2.4 and 3.5–3.7, which has no direct relationship to the underlying harmonies (essentially the same procedure seen in "Swing

'39" [example 5.2]), and the semitonally descending broken major thirds in mm. 3.1–3.2, an instance of chromaticism driven primarily by linear melodic considerations.

Similar "intentional wrong notes" can be heard throughout Reinhardt's recordings of the late 1940s. In example 5.6, from a solo on "Lady Be Good" (3/10/48; mx. OSW 501-1) recorded on the same day as "Bricktop," a glaring nonchord tone occurs on the final eighth note of m. 2.21. After arpeggiating a diminished-seventh chord over the secondary dominant A7 harmony, Reinhardt plays a G♯ in the guitar's upper register, a *major* seventh over a chord containing a minor seventh. This dissonance is not resolved until an A♮ appears on beat four of m. 2.22, more than three beats later at a moderate tempo of quarter note =

EXAMPLE 5.6. Improvisation on "Lady Be Good" (3/10/48; mx. OSW 501-1)

110. In the following two bars (mm. 2.23–2.24) Reinhardt plays a tritone substitution, articulating an A♭7 harmony over the dominant, D7; his use of this standard bebop convention will be discussed later.

Examples 5.7 and 5.8 illustrate two other unresolved dissonances. The first, from the beginning of a 1947 solo on "R-Vingt Six" (3/26/47; mx. OSW 449-1), contains a prominent A♯ in m. 2.2, a tritone from the root of the underlying E-minor harmony at the beginning of this measure. Instead of resolving the A♯ conventionally downward to A♮, which is the chord root in the second half of the same bar, Reinhardt follows it with B♮, the ninth of A. "Daphne" (1–2/49; mx. CW 34), the theme of the 1949 solo shown in example 5.8, is harmonically similar to "R-Vingt Six" and in the same key. M. 3.28 of "Daphne" contains another harmonic progression from E minor to A7, with Reinhardt playing an E♭, a tritone from the dominant's root. Not only does he leave the E♭ unresolved (unless the pitch D♮ occurring five beats later (not shown) is considered an extremely delayed resolution), but he approaches it by a leap of a melodic tritone (from the preceding A♮). While the guitarist has evidently absorbed the convention of tritone substitution sufficiently to use it improvisationally, its novelty value is still such that he seems to apply it as a self-conscious mannerism rather than integrating it more routinely into his playing.

These conspicuous unresolved nonharmonic tones indicate that for Reinhardt the late 1940s was a period of musical experimentation. This experimentalism also shaped his more harmonically oriented melodic

EXAMPLE 5.7. Improvisation on "R-Vingt Six" (3/26/47; mx. OSW 449-1)

EXAMPLE 5.8. Improvisation on "Daphne" (1–2/49; mx. CW 34)

procedures (usually implied by chord arpeggiations). Example 5.9 is from the guitarist's 1948 improvisation on "Mike" (3/10/48; mx. OSW 500-1), another original composition based on "I Got Rhythm" chord changes. The given extract is from the second half of a chorus, beginning with the eight-bar bridge. Although the bridge's harmonies are essentially those of "I Got Rhythm" in G major (a cycle of fifths, two bars per chord, arriving back on the tonic for the final A section), the bassist alternates between two quarter notes of each chord's root and two of its tritone partner. This explicit reference to a characteristic bebop interval seems unidiomatically exaggerated; in most contemporaneous American bebop it is quite uncommon for bassists to use tritones so explicitly and repetitiously. (Even the rare exceptions do not usually occur during an accompaniment to a solo but in a precomposed passage such as the introduction to Parker and Gillespie's 1945 composition "Shaw 'Nuff.") Reinhardt's solo contains a similarly mannered use of chromaticism. His first phrase during the bridge is quite routine harmonically—a rising arpeggiation of the underlying B-major chord followed by a mainly stepwise descent (mm. 3.17–3.19). But his next two bars, over an E7 har-

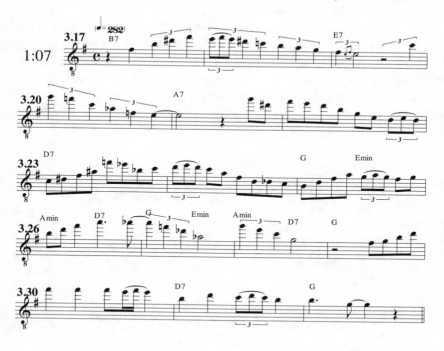

EXAMPLE 5.9. Improvisation on "Mike" (3/10/48; mx. OSW 500-1)

mony, contain a much greater range of dissonances. The series of pitches between the C♮ on the final quarter-note triplet of m. 3.19 and the downbeat of m. 3.21 suggests an F-minor harmony, with the G♮ apex pitch as an "upper-neighbor" prefix to F♮ (which is the accompanying harmony's minor ninth). A lower-octave F♮ resolves to the consonant E at the end of m. 3.20. (The A♭, which is enharmonically identical to G♯, of course belongs, like the E♮, to the underlying E-major chord.)

Reinhardt creates another unusual harmonic formation in m. 3.27 of the same solo. In this case a falling arpeggiation of a D♭-major triad, over chord changes of G major and E minor, is transposed a half step downward, resulting in a less dissonant arpeggiation of C major over the harmonies A minor and D7 (the pitches of a C-major triad all being members of an A-minor-seventh harmony). However, while the implied D♭-major over a G-major harmony is a tritone substitution, the final A♭ in m. 3.27, if respelled as G♯, functions as the *major* third of the underlying E-*minor* chord, an extremely unorthodox use of dissonance in jazz (or for that matter in any tonal music).[13]

Equally idiosyncratic harmonic procedures appear in a 1949 solo on "Lover Man" (1–2/49; mx. CW 37), from which example 5.10 is transcribed. This excerpt includes two passages that freely paraphrase the original melody, which are bracketed in the transcription. In m. 1.29, where the predetermined harmony is G minor, the guitarist first plays the ascending pitches F–A–C♯–E, which could be interpreted as the upper structure of a thirteenth chord with raised eleventh (i.e., the minor

EXAMPLE 5.10. Improvisation on "Lover Man" (1–2/49; mx. CW 37)

seventh, major ninth, sharpened eleventh, and thirteenth of G minor). Additionally, the B♮ on the fourth beat of the same bar is the chord's major third played over a minor harmony, as occurs in "Mike" (example 5.9). But what Reinhardt emphasizes most, by repetition, in m. 1.29 is the three-note augmented collection F–A–C♯. Then, in the next bar (m. 1.30), where the original harmony is a dominant seventh on C, he outlines a C-augmented harmony (C–E–G♯) on the downbeat and shifts swiftly on the second beat to a C-diminished collection (C–E♭–F♯), both of whose chord quality differs from the underlying C7, although they share the same root.

It did not take long for Reinhardt to advance beyond this sort of free experimentation and begin to master certain characteristic bebop melodic and harmonic techniques. His recordings document that by around 1948 he was using at least three such procedures quite consistently: (1) melodic resolution to scale degree 5 via scale degrees ♭7–♭6; (2) motion to the tonic note from scale degree ♭2 or ♭2–7; and (3) tritone substitution, particularly the substitution of the flat-supertonic harmony for the dominant (which is, of course, closely related to category 2).

Steven Strunk identifies melodic motion from scale degree ♭7 to ♭6 over a dominant harmony as a common bebop paradigm; it can also be thought of as motion from the minor tenth (often colloquially called a "raised ninth") to the minor ninth of the dominant. Strunk characterizes this phenomenon as a "tension" (more or less synonymous with "dissonance") that "find[s] resolution in a pitch other than a chord tone."[14] Steve Larson further notes that, after moving from scale degree ♭7 to ♭6, such melodies often resolve from scale degree ♭6 to 5.[15] Another similar, common configuration involves scale degree ♭6 resolving to 5 but with an intervening ♭7 functioning as an escape tone (again, this often occurs over a dominant chord), as seen at the beginning of m. 2.10 in example 5.11, from Charlie Parker's 1945 solo on "Now's the Time." Here, in the key of F major, the harmony is a dominant C7, and the melodic note D♭ resolves to C♮ with an intervening E♭ (in his taxonomy of Parker's formulas, Owens labels this melodic figure as motive M. 8).[16] Essentially the same melodic motion as in Parker's "Now's the Time" solo occurs in m. 2.3 of example 5.12, from Reinhardt's 1949 improvisation on "Hallelujah" (1–2/49; mx. CW 24): D♭ resolves to C♮ via the escape tone E♭. (The underlying harmony, however, is the tonic, F major, rather than the dominant.) Likewise, in m. 4.30 of example 5.13, another passage from the previously discussed solo on "Mike" (example 5.9), Reinhardt plays the pitch sequence F–E♭–D, corresponding in G major to scale degrees ♭7–♭6–5 (this figure resembles formula F17, given in chapter 3).

In m. 4.28 of example 5.13 Reinhardt implies a tritone substitution by playing E♭ and A♭, the fifth and root of an A♭ chord, over a D7 (dominant) harmony. With the arrival of the tonic harmony in m. 4.29, this substitution creates a descending half-step resolution of A♭ to G, scale degrees ♭2–1. Reinhardt often used both of these related bebop techniques during the final years of his career. Example 5.14, from his 1949 recording of "Beyond the Sea" (1–2/49; mx. CW 35), contains an equivalent procedure in mm. 2.12–2.13; again, he plays the root (G♭) and fifth (D♭) of the dominant (C) harmony's tritone partner (G♭ major) so that the tonic pitch, F, is approached via ♭2. Another variant on this resolution to the tonic, also common in bebop, is the phrase-ending melodic structure ♭2–7–1 (the tonic note preceded by its chromatic upper- and lower-

EXAMPLE 5.11. Scale degrees ♭6–♭7–5 from Charlie Parker's alto saxophone solo on "Now's the Time" (11/26/45)

EXAMPLE 5.12. Improvisation on "Hallelujah" (1–2/49; mx. CW 24)

EXAMPLE 5.13. Improvisation on "Mike" (3/10/48; mx. OSW 500-1)

neighbor notes in turn); DeVeaux calls this a "'Night in Tunisia' cadence" because it appears prominently in Gillespie's well-known composition "A Night in Tunisia."[17] Reinhardt uses it in m. 2.24–2.25 of his 1949 solo on "I Saw Stars" (1–2/49; mx. CW 52), shown in Example 5.15.

EXAMPLE 5.14. Improvisation on "Beyond the Sea" (1–2/49; mx. CW 35)

EXAMPLE 5.15. Improvisation on "I Saw Stars" (1–2/49; mx. CW 52)

Example 5.16, from Reinhardt's 1949 solo on Irving Berlin's "Marie" (1–2/49; mx. CW 38), displays a fairly extensive elaboration of a tritone substitution for the dominant. On the recording, the rhythm section (piano, bass, and drums) rests for almost four bars after playing an F-major (tonic) chord on the downbeat of m. 3.13; it reenters with an F7 harmony (m. 3.16) that tonicizes the subdominant, B♭, at the beginning of the chorus's second half (the form is a thirty-two-bar ABAC). During this four-bar break, Reinhardt precedes the F7 harmony with a rising and falling melodic gesture that arpeggiates G♭ major in mm. 3.14–3.15 (the two E♭s in m. 3.15 can be regarded as added sixths); G♭ major functions as a tritone substitution for the dominant, C major, harmony.[18] He furthermore approaches the arpeggiated G♭-major harmony with its own dominant, D♭, such that the original tonic (F-major) harmony in m. 3.13 is replaced with its flat-submediant harmony.

Two further instances of tritone substitution are illustrated in examples 5.17 and 5.18. Example 5.17, from a 1949 performance of "I Got Rhythm" (1–2/49; mx. CW 51), excerpts the eight-bar bridge—a descending-fifths progression. Reinhardt implies tritone substitutions simply by ending three of his phrases on notes a tritone away from the underlying chord roots in mm. 2.18, 2.22, and 2.24 (i.e., the note A♭ over a

EXAMPLE 5.16. Improvisation on "Marie" (1–2/49; mx. CW 38)

EXAMPLE 5.17. Improvisation on "I Got Rhythm" (1–2/49; mx. CW 51)

D7 harmony, G♭ over C7, and B♮ (C♭) over F7). Example 5.18, from a version of "Minor Swing" (1–2/49; mx. CW 40), also recorded in 1949, contains a more extensive rendering of the same substitution, with the substitute chord arpeggiated rather than implied by a single note. Here Reinhardt plays a rising arpeggiation of the flat-supertonic ("Neapolitan") harmony, B♭ major (m. 1.14), where the original harmony contains E7 (the dominant of A minor), but reverts to the diatonic B♮ at this gesture's apex.

Just how far Reinhardt's playing had evolved by the late 1940s can best be appreciated by comparing a solo from that period with one from the 1930s. Examples 5.19 and 5.20 are transcriptions of two improvisa-

EXAMPLE 5.18. Improvisation on "Minor Swing" (1–2/49; CW 40)

tions on "Honeysuckle Rose," the former recorded in 1938 and the latter in 1949 (the song has a thirty-two-bar AABA form). The 1938 version, featuring the Quintet of the Hot Club of France (1/31/38; mx. DTB 3523-1), contains one explicit musical discontinuity of the sort discussed in chapter 2, a quotation from Gershwin's *Rhapsody in Blue* played in octaves in mm. 2.12–2.15, and is replete with musical formulas. Especially marked chromaticism occurs at two points, both involving linear-oriented melodic figures. Mm. 2.8–2.10 contain a descending chromatic scale embellished with inverted-mordent ornaments, an instance of the formula F40 that contravenes the underlying chord changes, as do the intercalated descending chromatic scale segments in mm. 1.9–1.12, which are initiated by an instance of F13. The latter passage concludes with chromatic upper- and lower-neighbor notes prefixing the tonic pitch, F (mm.1.12–1.13), a figure resembling DeVeaux's "Night in Tunisia" cadence (with the order of the upper- and lower-neighbor notes reversed) and exemplifying the affinity between Reinhardt's swing era style and bebop.

The 1949 version of "Honeysuckle Rose" shows that once Reinhardt was exposed to bebop he not only used greater chromaticism but also adopted the new style's greater rhythmic complexity. His rhythmic strategies in the 1938 performance range from extremely symmetrical phrases, such as the strict repetition of a two-bar phrase in mm. 1.25–1.28, to subtle metric displacements, as in mm. 1.32–2.4, where ascending arpeggiations of a diminished-seventh harmony begin successively on beat three (m. 1.32), beat two (m. 2.2), and then the fourth eighth note of a measure (m. 2.4). The solo also contains instances of F39 (a motive reiterated at three-beat intervals) at mm. 1.19–1.21 and mm. 2.21–2.24. Reinhardt's 1949 solo (example 5.20, 1–2/49; mx. CW 29) con-

EXAMPLE 5.19. Improvisation on "Honeysuckle Rose" (1/31/38; mx. DTB 3523-1)

EXAMPLE 5.19. *(cont.)*

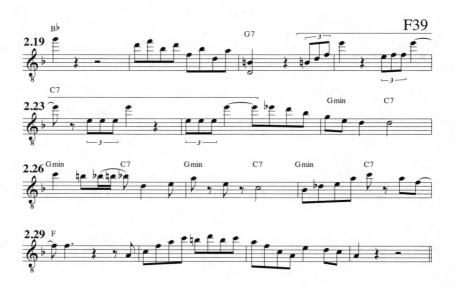

EXAMPLE 5.19. *(cont.)*

tains much more extreme syncopations and metric displacements. It opens with a three-beat-long rhythmic motive heard first on the downbeat of m. 2.1 and then on beat four of the same measure. This process repeats in mm. 2.3–2.4 with an altered melodic contour and the pitch G♭ substituting for G♮ (an alteration that accentuates the tritone partner of the underlying harmony's root (C♯); G♭ then resolves to the tonic note, F, on the downbeat of m. 2.5). F39, which appears in the 1938 version, is a precedent for this sort of metric displacement, although, being a context-specific formula, it usually occurs at the end of an eight-bar formal section. In example 5.20, by contrast, the displacements appear at the top of a chorus, making them more akin to the rhythmic scheme noted earlier in Reinhardt's composition "Babik (Bi-Bop)" and Parker's "Red Cross." Interestingly, the opening of the 1949 "Honeysuckle Rose" solo resembles—both rhythmically and in its melodic contours—a passage near the beginning of Parker's famous 1945 improvisation on "Ko Ko" (bars 5–8 of that solo), a recording that Reinhardt had probably heard.

Later in the 1949 solo, during his second chorus's bridge (mm. 3.17–3.24), Reinhardt creates even more radical syncopations and metric displacements. A four-part chord recurs sporadically throughout these measures, consisting of a major third, tritone, and perfect fourth stacked from bottom to top (the transcription has some enharmonic respellings).

EXAMPLE 5.20. Improvisation on "Honeysuckle Rose" (1–2/49; mx. CW 29)

Example 5.20. (cont.)

When playing this intervallic structure over an F7 harmony (m. 3.17), Reinhardt uses it to imply a thirteenth chord with augmented eleventh; over B♭7 (m. 3.19) and G7 (m. 3.21) it suggests a raised-ninth harmony; and against C7 (m. 3.23) it creates another thirteenth chord with augmented eleventh. The guitarist plays the four-part chords with a rhythmic asymmetry unparalleled in any of his recordings from the 1930s. In mm. 3.19 and 3.21 they occur, strongly accented, on beats three and four, framing a single-note melody that descends through the lower register with several eighth-note syncopations. During the bridge's final three bars (mm. 3.22–3.24) Reinhardt syncopates the four-part chords against the beat; he then introduces the last eight bars of the chorus with a series of quarter-note chords, moving in parallel motion, that begin two beats after the hypermetrical downbeat. Evidently these rhythmic irregularities risked confusing the accompanying rhythm section (piano, bass, and drums); to compensate, Reinhardt plays, from mm. 3.27–3.29, a descending melodic line in his instrument's lower register, arriving on the tonic note, F♮, at the downbeat of the chorus's final four bars (m. 3.29). This figure, probably intended to mimic a walking bass line, gives the rhythm section (particularly the bass player) an audible cue, helping it adhere to the music's underlying form despite the potential distraction of Reinhardt's many preceding syncopations.

The 1949 performance also contains clear tritone substitutions, such as at m. 3.18, where Reinhardt plays the perfect fifth G♭–C♭ (implying a C♭ harmony) over F7, and at m. 3.23, where he uses the fifth G♭–D♭ to suggest a G♭ chord over the underlying C7. Near the end of the first chorus (m. 2.28), the guitarist plays another tritone substitution in which the pitch G♭ appears over a dominant (C7) harmony as part of a "Night in Tunisia" cadence: G♭ and E function as chromatic neighbor-notes resolving to F in the next bar. Another bebop device in this solo is the melodic figure comprising scale degrees ♭7–♭6–5, which appears twice, in two different octaves, within the descending melodic line in mm. 2.5–2.6 and also in mm. 2.25–2.27.

The later "Honeysuckle Rose" solo also suggests that Reinhardt may have been listening to the recordings of Charlie Christian, the influential American electric guitarist who, before his death in 1942, was associated with the circle of musicians who invented bebop. The varied repetitions, in bars 3.3–3.12, of a short motive that arpeggiates downward from an upper-register F♮ are reminiscent of the riff-based melodies that were one of Christian's stylistic signatures. Since Reinhardt never played these sorts of phrases on his earlier recordings, they are likely another sign that he was gravitating toward new American musical trends during his late career.

It seems fitting to conclude this chapter with one of Reinhardt's final recordings. "Blues for Ike " (mx. 17276) dates from March 10, 1953, just two months before the guitarist died on May 16 of that year. On this, his penultimate recording session, Reinhardt was accompanied by young French musicians, including the bassist Pierre Michelot, one of the leading French jazz artists since World War II, who later worked with Americans such as the trumpeter Miles Davis, pianist Bud Powell, and saxophonist Dexter Gordon. "Blues for Ike," a twelve-bar blues transcribed in example 5.21, vividly illustrates how far Reinhardt's playing had evolved over the preceding decade. The guitar solo, which follows Michelot's two-chorus thematic exposition, features much bebop-flavored double-time (sixteenth-note) figuration, as well as overt tritone substitutions; in m. 1.12, Reinhardt emphasizes the note B♮ over the dominant harmony, F, and on the third beat of m. 5.8 he arpeggiates D♭ minor (♭III) near the end of his last chorus. The latter procedure creates the harmonic succession III–♭III–II in mm. 8–9 of the twelve-bar blues form, a typical bebop progression (♭III substitutes for a VI harmony, producing a chromatic passing chord between III and II instead of the cycle-of-fifths progression III–VI–II).

Along with these general bebop gestures, the solo reveals some apparent intersections between Reinhardt's earlier musical language and Parker's individual style. In both m. 4.1 and m. 4.3, the guitarist plays a series of sixteenth notes that includes the pitches E–G–B♭–D♭–C (a rising diminished-seventh arpeggiation followed by a half-step descent, which begins on the third note of each passage). This figure is nearly identical to one of Parker's most common melodic formulas (Owens labels it M. 1Ba),[19] and it also resembles the guitarist's own formula F4 (compare, specifically, F4c from Figure 3.1), which he was using during the 1930s. During that earlier decade, however, Reinhardt ordinarily played this formula in a higher register and typically preceded it with an initial diminished-seventh arpeggiation encompassing more than the single octave seen here. Reinhardt may have adapted his own formula so that it more closely resembled one of Parker's.

"Blues for Ike" also mirrors Parker's use of sporadic, overtly blues-based interjections. These interjections, which feature the minor pentatonic scale and often involve bent blue notes, include the eighth-note passage in mm. 3.1–3.2, with scale degree ♭3 emphasized on the down-

EXAMPLE 5.21. Improvisation on "Blues for Ike" (3/10/53; mx. 17276)

EXAMPLE 5.21. *(cont.)*

EXAMPLE 5.21. *(cont.)*

beat of m. 3.2; mm. 4.5–4.6, where the phrase's apex pitch is the flattened-fifth scale degree, another blue note; and mm. 4.12–5.3, where the guitarist begins his final chorus by "choking" with his left hand on the fretboard so as to sound the pitch D♮ by sharpening the D♭ (scale degree ♭3) a half-step beneath it (indicated in the transcription by the short oblique lines on either side of the note head). Parker frequently uses these sorts of abrupt shifts between comparatively chromatic harmony and pentatonic blues figures, but Reinhardt rarely does so in his early work; even the minor-pentatonic passage in his "Swing '39" solo (example 5.2) sounds less blues oriented because it involves a harmonic displacement rather than a melodic superimposition.

There are even some apparent connections between "Blues for Ike" and one of Parker's specific solos, "Parker's Mood," which is also a twelve-bar blues in B♭ major. It is quite likely that Reinhardt knew

Parker's 1948 recording, which was one of the saxophonist's most widely acclaimed performances.[20] Bars 9–10 of each of Parker's choruses contain a chromatic descent from the pitch D♮ through B♭ (this resembles a formula that Owens labels M. 4Ea and is also a subunit of Owens's M. 13Aa).[21] In each case, the saxophonist embellishes the note B♭ with a complete upper-neighbor note and then continues the melodic descent.[22] (As noted, Owens identifies these sorts of melodic descents as a key stylistic trait of Parker's.) Reinhardt's solo, too, contains chromatic descents from D♮ through an ornamented B♭ in approximately the same formal location (mm. 3.9–3.10 and 4.10).

For all its progressive bebop elements, "Blues for Ike" displays many continuities with Reinhardt's swing era playing; the guitarist's postwar evolution involved no radical stylistic break like that between his early musette playing and his music of the 1930s. His late style retains, for instance, much of his earlier formulaic vocabulary, though with many modifications. As well as reworking the formula F4, he adapted the superformula F36, which during the 1930s and 1940s generally articulated an ascending triadic arpeggiation with a turn around each primary (consonant) note. In m. 3.8 of "Blues for Ike," F36 retains its upper- and lower-neighbor-note embellishments but shifts in midstream from its typical arpeggiated ascent to a stepwise one. The pitches being ornamented are thus (D)–F–B♭–C–D–(F). While this formula was formerly quite invariant ("fixed"), it is now treated relatively flexibly.

Reinhardt's death at forty-three cut short an ongoing creative odyssey. Scarcely any other swing era jazz improvisers made comparable mid-career decisions to dramatically transform their postwar musical languages, and the guitarist's untimely passing left open some tantalizing questions. Within only a few years the jazz world witnessed many more stylistic changes. Would Reinhardt have recast his playing again in response to these trends? Or would he eventually have returned to the acoustic guitar and his earlier style? While we shall never know where his artistic evolution might have led, it is safe to say that his legacy, from the early musette recordings through the era of the Quintet to the final bebop years, encompasses a stylistic range that has few, if any, parallels among his contemporaries.

EPILOGUE

ver half a century has now passed since Django Reinhardt died, and his music endures through his lingering influence on today's players, in an ongoing stream of tribute concerts and festivals, and above all in his hundreds of recordings. As jazz's first major non-American artist, he personifies the idiom's worldwide impact. While it has always possessed special social functions and meanings for its African American inventors, jazz has also, for nearly its entire history, flourished far from its original cultural setting, profoundly shaping the lives of other peoples in other ways. That a European such as Reinhardt has become a canonic figure is as much a testament to black Americans' global achievement as it is to his individual artistry.

This book has dealt with only a few aspects of this artistry, and even within its limited scope it leaves many issues unresolved. Among the most pressing is how Reinhardt's playing relates to that of other jazz improvisers of his day. I have not, for instance, determined how widespread the musical discontinuities discussed in chapter 2 are other than to note anecdotally that several other players occasionally used such techniques. These sorts of comparative issues have only been addressed here in a few narrow cases such as in chapter 1's contrasting of Reinhardt's left-hand technique with Eddie Lang's or chapter 5's assessment of the way bebop players such as Charlie Parker influenced the guitarist late in his career. Further context is lacking simply because to date so little analytical research has been conducted on jazz.[1] Chapter 3's discussion of Reinhardt's melodic formulas, for example, draws on a mere handful of prior studies of formulaic improvisation in jazz, of which only one—Thomas Owens's nonpareil work on Parker—even attempts to gain a comprehensive understanding of this dimension of a single player's improvisational process. (That Parker continues to be characterized as "the greatest formulaic improviser in jazz" may well be mainly an indication that no similarly thorough research has been carried out on any other musician.)[2]

A deeper understanding and appreciation of Reinhardt's musical legacy therefore awaits not only further scholarship on the guitarist himself but the broader perspective that will emerge once more is known about the playing of his contemporaries. At this writing there are still no extensive published studies of the music of Coleman Hawkins, Johnny Hodges, Roy Eldridge, or Benny Carter, to name just a few other leading swing era soloists.[3] These figures, like Reinhardt and many others, dedicated themselves to a music that richly deserves to be confronted in all its fine detail and subtle intricacy, and that has yet to receive its due.

◉ NOTES ◉

PREFACE

1. LeRoi Jones [Amiri Baraka], "Jazz and the White Critic," in *Black Music* (New York: Da Capo, 1998), 15; first published in 1963. Jones/Baraka's argument is in part a riposte to the writings of André Hodeir and Gunther Schuller, whose analytical work of the 1950s, particularly Hodeir's, will be further discussed in this book. The evolution of jazz theory and analysis, including some pre-1950 precedents, is surveyed in Henry Martin, "Jazz Theory: An Overview," *Annual Review of Jazz Studies* 8 (1996): 1–17; and Thomas Owens, "Analysing Jazz," in *The Cambridge Companion to Jazz,* ed. Mervyn Cooke and David Horn (Cambridge: Cambridge University Press, 2002), 286–97.

2. John Gennari, *Blowin' Hot and Cool: Jazz and its Critics* (Chicago: University of Chicago Press, 2006), 4.

3. Michael Tenzer, "Introduction: Analysis, Categorization, and Theory of Musics of the World," in *Analytical Studies in World Music,* ed. Michael Tenzer (New York: Oxford University Press, 2006), 9.

4. John Covach, "We Won't Get Fooled Again: Rock Music and Musical Analysis," in *Keeping Score: Music, Interdisciplinarity, and Culture,* ed. David Schwarz, Anahid Kassabian, and Lawrence Siegel (Charlottesville: University of Virginia Press, 1997), 83.

5. Other primarily analytical monographs on single jazz artists include Charles Blancq, *Sonny Rollins: The Journey of a Jazzman* (Boston: Twayne, 1983); Lewis Porter, *Lester Young,* rev. ed. (Ann Arbor: University of Michigan Press, 2005); Carl Woideck, *Charlie Parker: His Music and Life* (Ann Arbor: University of Michigan Press, 1996); and Henry Martin, *Charlie Parker and Thematic Improvisation* (Lanham, MD: Scarecrow, 1996).

INTRODUCTION

1. By his midthirties, Reinhardt was able to write a four-page letter, idiosyncratically spelled and in block capitals, to Stéphane Grappelli while touring the United States with the Duke Ellington Orchestra in 1946. See Stéphane Grap-

pelli with Joseph Oldenhove and Jean-Marc Bramy, *Mon Violon pour Tout Bagage: Mémoires* (Paris: Calmann-Lévy, 1992), plate following p. 112; and Paul Balmer, *Stéphane Grappelli: With and without Django* (London: Sanctuary, 2003), plate facing p. 129.

2. The best biographies of Reinhardt are probably Charles Delaunay, *Django Reinhardt,* trans. Michael James (New York: Da Capo, 1981 [1961]); Patrick Williams, *Django Reinhardt* (Marseilles: Éditions Parenthèses, 1998); François Billard, *Django Reinhardt: Un géant sur son nuage* (Paris: Lieu Commun, 1993); and Michael Dregni, *Django: The Life and Music of a Gypsy Legend* (New York: Oxford University Press, 2004).

3. The most comprehensive discography of Reinhardt's recordings is Paul Vernon, *Jean "Django" Reinhardt: A Contextual Bio-discography, 1910–1953* (Aldershot: Ashgate, 2003). Although recordings are the main musical documents available, they are certainly far from ideal historical sources. See Jed Rasula, "The Media of Memory: The Seductive Menace of Records in Jazz History," in *Jazz among the Discourses,* ed. Krin Gabbard (Durham: Duke University Press, 1995), 134–62.

4. Dregni, *Django,* 13–16.

5. William A. Shack, *Harlem in Montmartre: A Paris Jazz Story between the Great Wars* (Berkeley: University of California Press, 2000), 28. Also see Jeffrey Green, "'In Dahomey' in London in 1903," *The Black Perspective in Music* 11/1 (spring 1983): 22–40.

6. See Jeffrey H. Jackson, *Making Jazz French: Music and Modern Life in Interwar Paris* (Durham: Duke University Press, 2003), 18.

7. See Tyler Stovall, *Paris Noir: African Americans in the City of Light* (Boston: Mariner, 1996), 25–81.

8. Shack, *Harlem in Montmartre,* 24–25; Delaunay, *Django Reinhardt,* 40; Dregni, *Django,* 40.

9. Ernest Ansermet, "Sur un Orchestre Nègre," *Revue Romande,* October 1919, reprinted in *Keeping Time: Readings in Jazz History,* ed. Robert Walser (New York: Oxford University Press, 1999), 9–11.

10. For details, see Sidney Bechet, *Treat It Gentle* (New York: Da Capo, 2002 [1960]), 149–56.

11. See, for instance, Jack Sullivan, *New World Symphonies: How American Culture Changed European Music* (New Haven: Yale University Press, 1999), 191–237; Roger Nichols, *The Harlequin Years: Music in Paris, 1917–1929* (Berkeley: University of California Press, 2002); and Richard Taruskin, *The Oxford History of Western Music* (New York: Oxford University Press, 2005), 4:561–613.

12. Jackson, *Making Jazz French,* 123–53.

13. Ibid., 124.

14. Ibid., 143–53.

15. André Hodeir, *Jazz: Its Evolution and Essence,* trans. David Noakes (New York: Grove, 1956), 196. "Swing," in Hodeir's view, involves a simultaneous sense of tension and relaxation created by combining the right tempo and metrical structure with certain types of melodic syncopation and accents (195–209);

"hot playing" is an energetic, loud performance style (230–33). For a short biographical sketch see André Hodeir, *The André Hodeir Jazz Reader*, ed. Jean-Louis Pautrot (Ann Arbor: University of Michigan Press, 2006), 3–11.

16. Scott DeVeaux, for example, takes the view that defining jazz "is easier if one bypasses the usual inventory of musical qualities or techniques" by focusing instead on "issues of ethnicity and economics [that] define jazz as an oppositional discourse: the music of an oppressed minority culture, tainted by its association with commercial entertainment in a society that reserves its greatest respect for art that is carefully removed from daily life" ("Constructing the Jazz Tradition," in *The Jazz Cadence of American Culture*, ed. Robert G. O'Meally [New York: Columbia University Press, 1998], 486–87). Likewise, William Howland Kenney writes that "attention to historical context . . . reveals far better than aural evidence that jazz involved a set of specific social, economic, and racial experiences among those who performed it and those who eagerly listened to it" ("Historical Context and the Definition of Jazz: Putting More of the History in 'Jazz History,'" in *Jazz among the Discourses*, ed. Krin Gabbard [Durham: Duke University Press, 1995], 112).

17. Rex Stewart, *Boy Meets Horn*, ed. Claire P. Gordon (Ann Arbor: University of Michigan Press, 1991), 186.

18. Rich Kienzle, *Great Guitarists* (New York: Facts on File, 1985), 116; Mary Alice Shaughnessey, *Les Paul: An American Original* (New York: Morrow, 1993), 135–36, 209; Bill Lee, "Barney Kessel," in *Jazz Guitarists: Collected Interviews from Guitar Player Magazine* (Saratoga, CA: Guitar Player Productions, 1975), 78.

19. Don Menn, ed., *Secrets from the Masters: Conversations with Forty Great Guitar Players* (San Francisco: Miller Freeman, 1992), 160; Chet Atkins with Bill Neely, *Country Gentleman* (Chicago: Regnery, 1974), 78; Jas Obrecht, ed., *Rollin' and Tumblin': The Postwar Blues Guitarists* (San Francisco: Miller Freeman, 2000), 320, 327, 337; B. B. King with David Ritz, *Blues All around Me: The Autobiography of B. B. King* (New York: Avon, 1996), 104–5, quoted in Michael Dregni, *Gypsy Jazz: In Search of Django Reinhardt and the Soul of Gypsy Swing* (New York: Oxford University Press, 2008), 8; Steve Rosen, "Mahavishnu John McLaughlin," in *Jazz Guitarists: Collected Interviews from Guitar Player Magazine* (Saratoga, CA: Guitar Player Productions, 1975), 72; Menn, *Secrets from the Masters*, 218, 198.

20. Regarding the imitative impulse, see John Jorgenson, "Django for a Day," *Acoustic Guitar* July 2004, 36–42.

21. Hear, for example, Lagrène's recent albums, *Gypsy Project* (Dreyfus 36626, 2001), *Gipsy Project and Friends* (Dreyfus 36638, 2002), *Move* (Dreyfus 36668, 2005), and *Djangology/To Bi or Not to Bi* (Dreyfus 36695, 2007).

22. "Django ne joue *pas* style gitan. Il joue un style qui luis est propre. La musique de Django commence avec lui-même. Il joue certes de la guitare, instrument traditionnel, mais il a fait lui même son école de guitar. Il a crée un style. Cette école part de lui" (Michel-Claude Jalard, "Django et l'école tsigane du jazz," *Les Cahiers du Jazz* 1 [1959], quoted in Ekkehard Jost, "Jazz, Musette,

und Cante Flamenco: Traditionslinen in der Musik der französischen Gitans und Manouches," in *Die Musik der Sinti und Roma,* vol. 2: *Der Sinti-Jazz,* ed. Anita Awosusi [Heidelberg: Schriftenreihe des Dokumentations- und Kulturzentrums Deutscher Sinti und Roma, 1997], 16).

23. See, for instance, Michael Dregni with Alain Antonietto and Anne Legrand, *Django Reinhardt and the Illustrated History of Gypsy Jazz* (Denver: Speck, 2006); and Dregni, *Gypsy Jazz,* ix–xii and passim.

24. The classic text on "invented tradition" is *The Invention of Tradition,* ed. Eric Hobsbawm and Terence Ranger (Cambridge: Cambridge University Press, 1983). The construction of a "gypsy jazz" tradition mirrors the way historians have constructed the core jazz tradition, as discussed in DeVeaux, "Constructing the Jazz Tradition."

25. To give just one recent example, Geoffrey C. Ward and Ken Burns's jazz history book (which accompanies Burns's television documentary) discusses Reinhardt in a section, entitled "The Gypsy," that focuses heavily on exotic (and in some cases factually dubious) elements of the guitarist's biography such as his mother's dark complexion, his "wandering" nature, his supposed gastronomical predilection for roasted hedgehog, and so forth (*Jazz: A History of America's Music* [New York: Knopf, 2000], 299).

26. Patrick Williams, *Gypsy World: The Silence of the Living and the Voices of the Dead,* trans. Catherine Tihanyi (Chicago: University of Chicago Press, 2003), passim.

27. Ibid., 88.

CHAPTER 1

1. Until recently, most sources gave the date of Reinhardt's accident as November 2, 1928, but recently evidence has come to light indicating the earlier date. See Paul Balmer, *Stéphane Grappelli: With and without Django* (London: Sanctuary, 2003), 70; and Michael Dregni, *Django: The Life and Music of a Gypsy Legend* (New York: Oxford University Press, 2004), 45–48. Other biographical details presented here are drawn from Charles Delaunay, *Django Reinhardt,* trans. Michael James (New York: Da Capo, 1981 [1961]), 43–55; François Billard, *Django Reinhardt: Un géant sur son nuage* (Paris: Lieu Commun, 1993), 53–58; and Patrick Williams, *Django Reinhardt* (Marseilles: Éditions Parenthèses, 1998), 15–16.

2. Jody Blake, *Le Tumulte noir: Modernist Art and Popular Entertainment in Jazz-Age Paris, 1900–1930* (University Park: Pennsylvania State University Press, 1999), 102–5.

3. Alain Antonietto, "La Main de Django," *Études Tsiganes* 2 (1984): 41–48, discussed in Williams, *Django Reinhardt,* 25.

4. Billard, *Django Reinhardt,* 58.

5. Delaunay reports that Reinhardt was first introduced to the records of

jazz violinist Joe Venuti (and probably also, by implication, Venuti's frequent collaborator Eddie Lang) by Emile Savitry around 1930 (*Django Reinhardt,* 47).

6. Quoted in Richard M. Sudhalter, *Lost Chords: White Musicians and Their Contribution to Jazz, 1915–1945* (New York: Oxford University Press, 1999), 534.

7. Dregni, *Django,* 86.

8. Ian Cruickshank, *The Guitar Style of Django Reinhardt and the Gypsies* (London: Wise , 1989), 6; Mike Peters, liner notes to *The Complete Django Reinhardt and Quintet of the Hot Club of France Swing/HMV Sessions, 1936–1948* (Mosaic Records MD6-190, 1999), 2.

9. Mike Zwerin, "Jazz in Europe," in *The Oxford Companion to Jazz,* ed. Bill Kirchner (New York: Oxford University Press, 2000), 539; Geoffrey Smith, *Stéphane Grappelli* (London: Pavilion, 1987), 50; Raymond Horricks, *Stéphane Grappelli* (Tunbridge Wells: Baton, 1983), 17; Marc-Edouard Nabe, *Nuage* (Paris: Le Dilettante, 1993), 23; Dregni, *Django,* 46.

10. Michael James with Howard Rye and Barry Kernfeld, "Django Reinhardt," in *The New Grove Dictionary of Jazz,* 2nd ed., ed. Barry Kernfeld (New York: Macmillan, 2002), 3: 396.

11. "Il lui restera . . . le handicap . . . de ne pouvoir faire les notes sur le manche qu'avec trois doigts, le médium, l'index et le pouce" (Williams, *Django Reinhardt,* 16).

12. Raoul Tubiana and Philippe Chamagne, "Functional Anatomy of the Hand," *Medical Problems of Performing Artists* 3/3 (September 1988): 84–86.

13. Raoul Tubiana, "Movements of the Fingers," *Medical Problems of Performing Artists* 3/4 (December 1988): 124.

14. George H. Koepke, Barbara Feallock, and Irving Feller, "Splinting the Severely Burned Hand," *American Journal of Occupational Therapy* 17 (1963): 147.

15. H. Minor Nichols, *Manual of Hand Injuries* (Chicago: Year Book, 1955), 97.

16. Ibid., 109.

17. John A. Boswick Jr., "Rehabilitation of the Burned Hand," *Clinical Orthapaedics* 104 (1974): 171.

18. A close-up photograph of Reinhardt's hand is reproduced in a previously published version of this chapter (Benjamin Givan, "Django Reinhardt's Left Hand," in *Jazz Planet,* ed. E. Taylor Atkins [Jackson: University Press of Mississippi, 2003], 24).

19. Billy Neill and E. Gates, *Discography of the Recorded Works of Django Reinhardt and the Quintette du Hot Club de France* (London: Clifford Essex Music, 1944), quoted in George Hoefer, "Django Reinhardt: The Magnificent Gypsy," *Down Beat,* July 1966, 22, emphasis in the original. Neill's and Gates's claim that by playing octaves on two strings with a damped intervening string Reinhardt avoided "rushing up and down the fingerboard" seems misplaced since this fingering would still require a good deal of such movement.

20. *Melody Maker,* March 13, 1954, quoted in Delaunay, *Django Reinhardt,* 17.

21. Mike Peters, "Teach-In: Django Reinhardt," *Sing Out!* 29/1 (1982): 12.

22. Whitney Balliett, "Seeing Music," *New Yorker,* September 11, 2000, 99. It is possible that the accounts of both Peters and Balliett may be based on a reading of Grappelli's description, cited here, since it appears in Delaunay's book, which (in translation) was until recently the most widely circulated biography of Reinhardt in English. Another source is the American guitarist Art Ryerson, who states, "[Reinhardt's] third finger wasn't a hundred percent, but he could use it about two-thirds of the time, and he could even use the damaged fourth once in a while" (quoted in Sudhalter, *Lost Chords,* 534).

23. Alexander Schmitz and Peter Maier, *Django Reinhardt: Sein Leben, Seine Musik, Seine Schallplatten* (Buchendorf: Oreos Verlag, 1985), 57–60.

24. "Djangos Ringfinger der linken hand war fast immer dann komplett nutzbar, wenn zwischen ihm und dem Mittelfinger keine allzu große Streckung erforderlich war" (ibid., 57–58).

25. *Supination* describes the rotation of the wrist in the direction that brings the palm uppermost; its antonym is *pronation,* in which the wrist is rotated in the direction bringing the palm face-down (and beyond). See Ivan Galamian, *Principles of Violin Playing and Teaching* (Englewood Cliffs, NJ: Prentice-Hall, 1962), 50; and Raoul Tubiana, "Anatomy of the Hand and Upper Limb," in *Medical Problems of the Instrumentalist Musician,* ed. Raoul Tubiana and Peter C. Amadio (London: Dunitz, 2000), 13.

26. Schmitz and Maier, *Django Reinhardt,* 57.

27. The complete film, which lasts six and a half minutes, became commercially available for the first time as part of some supplementary material included on the recent DVD documentary *Stéphane Grappelli: A Life in the Jazz Century* (Music on Earth 001, 2002).

28. One such photograph is reproduced in Givan, "Django Reinhardt's Left Hand," 27.

29. Most famously, Gennett studios in Richmond, Indiana, where Louis Armstrong made some of his first recordings with King Oliver's Creole Jazz Band during the early 1920s, used a turntable that spun slightly too fast (Rick Kennedy, *Jelly Roll, Bix, and Hoagy: Gennett Studios and the Birth of Recorded Jazz* [Bloomington: Indiana University Press, 1994], 30). As a result the pitch (and tempo) of these recordings is slightly low (and slow) when played back on a properly calibrated phonograph.

30. Throughout this book, recordings are identified by their dates and matrix numbers (the unique reference numbers the record company assigns to each separate take).

31. See Jay Scott Odell and Robert B. Winans, "Banjo," in *The New Grove Dictionary of Music and Musicians,* 2nd ed., ed. Stanley Sadie (London: Macmillan, 2001), 2: 662. The numerals used here refer to specific registers; by convention, middle C and the notes within the octave above it are described as C4, C♯4, D4, and so forth. The pitches one octave higher are indicated by the number 5, the octave below middle C by the number 3, and so forth.

32. See, for instance, the prescribed use of the left thumb in John Jorgenson, "Gypsy Guitar Primer," *Acoustic Guitar,* February 1996, 40–42.

33. Both this and the performance transcribed in example 1.4 are extremely free glosses on Lao Silèsu's theme as it was originally published, and in both cases their rubato tempi are difficult to capture in musical notation. This difficulty has no ramifications for the present discussion, however.

34. With regard to the transcription of Lang's performance, it should be noted that he frequently arpeggiates four-, five-, and six-note chords. When these are played slowly, the pitches are notated with individual rhythmic values. When a note within any such chord continues to sound (i.e., the string continues to be depressed by the left hand), this is indicated in the left-hand fingering notation with the use of a horizontal line (e.g., in m. 2). In a few, mostly self-evident, cases I have omitted these lines in the interest of visual clarity.

35. Example 1.6b shows only one of several possible fingerings for this passage.

36. See, for instance, Ben Ratliff, "A Delirium of Gypsy Music Barrels Along in Overdrive," *New York Times,* December 4, 2000, E5.

37. Gunther Schuller, *The Swing Era: The Development of Jazz, 1930–1945* (New York: Oxford University Press, 1989), 564–66.

38. The guitarist Mary Osborne recalled hearing Christian play Reinhardt's recorded solo on "St. Louis Blues" (see example 2.2) note for note at a concert date in Bismarck, North Dakota, during the late 1930s (Leonard Ferris, "Mary Osborne: A Unique Roll [*sic*] in Jazz Guitar History," in *Jazz Guitarists: Collected Interviews from* Guitar Player *Magazine* [Saratoga, CA: Guitar Player Productions, 1975], 78).

39. For instance, in a *Down Beat* magazine poll of January 1939 Reinhardt ranked fifteenth in the guitar category. Those ahead of him included Allen Reuss, Teddy Bunn, Eddie Condon, George Van Eps, and Freddie Green. The top three winners were, in order, Benny Heller (with Benny Goodman), Carmen Mastren (with Tommy Dorsey), and Nappy Lamare (with Bob Crosby), three artists who, needless to say, no longer enjoy such lofty reputations ("Final Results of Band Contest," *Down Beat,* January 1939, 17). In the following year Charlie Christian, having reached a wider audience after joining the Benny Goodman Orchestra, placed first in the guitar poll with Reinhardt ranked twentieth ("11 Leaders on *Down Beat's* All-American 1939 Band," *Down Beat,* January 1, 1940, 13).

40. This point is noted in Rob van der Bliek, "Wes Montgomery: A Study of Coherence in Jazz Improvisation," *Jazzforschung* 23 (1991): 151–52. Alexander Schmitz points out that Reinhardt's technique of playing octaves by stretching a distance of three frets between two strings with one (damped) intervening string, later adopted by Montgomery, differs from the octave fingering often favored by classical guitarists whereby there are *two* intervening strings between the sounding strings and the fingering (e.g., the first and third fingers) involves a heavily supinated wrist (Alexander Schmitz, "Stilprägende Elemente in der Musik von Django Reinhardt," in *Die Musik der Sinti und Roma,* vol. 2: *Der Sinti-Jazz,* ed. Anita Awosusi [Heidelberg: Schriftenreihe des Dokumentations- und Kulturzentrums Deutscher Sinti und Roma, 1997], 34).

CHAPTER 2

1. André Hodeir, *Jazz: Its Evolution and Essence,* trans. David Noakes (New York: Grove, 1956); Gunther Schuller, "Sonny Rollins and the Challenge of Thematic Improvisation," *Jazz Review* 1/1 (November 1958): 6–11, 21, reprinted in Gunther Schuller, *Musings: The Musical Worlds of Gunther Schuller* (New York: Oxford University Press, 1986), 86–97. For a discussion of Hodeir's and Schuller's ideological motivations, see Robert Walser, "Deep Jazz: Notes on Race, Interiority, and Criticism," in *Inventing the Psychological: Toward a Cultural History of Emotional Life in America,* ed. Joel Pfister and Nancy Schnog (New Haven: Yale University Press, 1997), 271–96.

2. Henry Martin compares Charlie Parker's improvisations to "the understated perfection of a Chopin *Waltz,* Debussy or Bach *Prelude,* or Schubert *Impromptu*" in that they exemplify "the subtlest fine-art desiderata" (*Charlie Parker and Thematic Improvisation* [Lanham, MD: Scarecrow, 1996], 129–30). And Steve Larson has written that "Schenkerian analysis may be applied to any jazz performance—and it may show the shortcomings of that performance" ("Schenkerian Analysis of Modern Jazz," *Music Theory Spectrum* 20/2 [1998]: 241). On another occasion Larson noted that "the sophisticated relationships prized by music analysts appear in the music of Bill Evans—and in the music of Bach and Brahms" ("Composition versus Improvisation?" *Journal of Music Theory* 49/2 [2005]: 273).

3. See, for instance, Gary Tomlinson, "Cultural Dialogics and Jazz: A White Historian Signifies," in *Disciplining Music,* ed. Katherine Bergeron and Philip V. Bohlman (Chicago: University of Chicago Press, 1992), 64–94; Robert Walser, "Out of Notes: Signification, Interpretation, and the Problem of Miles Davis," in *Jazz among the Discourses,* ed. Krin Gabbard (Durham: Duke University Press, 1995), 165–88; and Samuel A. Floyd Jr., *The Power of Black Music: Interpreting Its History from Africa to the United States* (New York: Oxford University Press, 1995).

4. Ingrid Monson, *Saying Something: Jazz Improvisation and Interaction* (Chicago: University of Chicago Press, 1996), 186, 190.

5. Whitney Balliett, "Seeing Music," *New Yorker,* September 11, 2000, 99.

6. André Hodeir, *Toward Jazz,* trans. Noel Burch (New York: Grove, 1962), 188, originally published in *Jazz Hot* 88 (May 1954).

7. For example, clarinetist Pee Wee Russell states, "I usually think about four bars ahead what I'm going to play"; flugelhorn player Art Farmer observes, "I rarely know what I'm going to do in a solo more than a measure or two ahead"; and tenor saxophonist Warne Marsh claims, "My mind works ahead a bar or two" (quoted in Whitney Balliett, *American Musicians II: Seventy-two Portraits in Jazz* [New York: Oxford University Press 1996], 138, 447, 492).

8. Balliett, "Seeing Music," 98.

9. For instance, the vibraphonist Milt Jackson has said, "I keep the melody in mind. I always remember the melody and then I have something to fall back on when I get lost" (quoted in Balliett, *American Musicians II,* 308). The pianist

Hank Jones stated, "[Y]ou think about the chord pattern—not each chord—and you think about the melody" (quoted in Whitney Balliett, *Collected Works: A Journal of Jazz, 1954–2000* [New York: St. Martin's, 2000], 837).

10. Hodeir, *Jazz,* 144.

11. Lawrence Gushee, "Lester Young's Shoe Shine Boy," in *Report of the Twelfth Congress, Berkeley, 1977,* International Musicological Society, ed. Daniel Heartz and Bonnie Wade (Kassel: Bärenreiter, 1981), 158.

12. For refinements of Hodeir's scheme, see Barry Kernfeld, "Adderley, Coltrane, and Davis at the Twilight of Bebop: The Search for Melodic Coherence (1958–59)," PhD diss., Cornell University, 1981, 17; Barry Kernfeld, *What to Listen For in Jazz* (New Haven: Yale University Press, 1995), 131; and Martin, *Charlie Parker and Thematic Improvisation,* 34. For a critique, see Steve Larson, "Swing and Motive in Three Performances by Oscar Peterson," *Journal of Music Theory* 43/2 (1999): 286. I discuss Kernfeld's and Martin's writings on this topic in Benjamin Givan, "Jazz Taxonomies," *Jazz Research News* 10 (March 2003): 476–80.

13. One could, of course, add to this list by including phenomena such as the "moment form," codified in the writings of Karlheinz Stockhausen (for a summary, see Jonathan Kramer, "Moment Form in Twentieth Century Music," *Musical Quarterly* 64 [1978]: 177–94), or various postmodern "collage" techniques. Even the romantic (or modernist) notion of organicism can be conceived in dialectical terms, for example, as the synthesis of contrasting ideas. See Michael Cherlin, "Dialectical Opposition in Schoenberg's Music and Thought," *Music Theory Spectrum* 22/2 (2000): 157–76.

14. This is discussed in Albert Murray, *Stomping the Blues* (New York: McGraw-Hill, 1976), 94.

15. Edward T. Cone, "Stravinsky: The Progress of a Method," in *Music: A View from Delft: Selected Essays,* ed. Robert P. Morgan (Chicago: University of Chicago Press, 1989), 294.

16. Gunther Schuller, *The Swing Era: The Development of Jazz, 1930–1945* (New York: Oxford University Press, 1989), 280.

17. Paul Berliner, *Thinking in Jazz: The Infinite Art of Improvisation* (Chicago: University of Chicago Press, 1994), 195. Berliner also identifies similar usages in the work of saxophonist Lester Young and trumpeter Miles Davis (574).

18. This is discussed in Gary Giddins, *Satchmo* (New York: Dolphin, 1988), 127. I address Armstrong's use of such techniques in Benjamin Givan, "Duets for One: Louis Armstrong's Vocal Recordings," *Musical Quarterly* 87/2 (summer 2004): 188–218.

19. Charles O. Hartman, *Jazz Text: Voice and Improvisation in Poetry, Jazz, and Song* (Princeton: Princeton University Press, 1991), 111. For a list of some baroque works that feature compound melodic lines, see Albert S. Bregman, *Auditory Scene Analysis: The Perceptual Organization of Sound* (Cambridge: MIT Press, 1990), 463.

20. Cone, "Stravinsky," 295.

21. A strict, practically viable definition of melodic paraphrase in jazz im-

provisation has eluded jazz scholars for reasons illustrated by example 2.6; performers often utilize paraphrase very freely. For a brief discussion of this issue, see J. Kent Williams, "Authors' Responses to Forte's Questions," *Annual Review of Jazz Studies* 9 (1997–98): 104–5. For instance, Brian Harker cites Louis Armstrong's diminishing differentiation between melodic paraphrases and arpeggiated, harmonically oriented improvised melodies as a feature of the trumpeter's stylistic evolution during the mid- to late 1920s ("'Telling a Story': Louis Armstrong and Coherence in Early Jazz," *Current Musicology* 63 [1999]: 58.).

22. The term *structural marker* is used by Berliner in *Thinking in Jazz.*

23. Musical accompaniments in a variety of genres are often characterized by the repetition of short musical units. In the terminology of Gestalt psychology, repetitive accompaniments constitute a "ground" against which a listener can individuate a foregrounded melodic "figure."

24. In the present context the terms *foreground* and *background* ought not to be confused with the same terms as they are used in Schenkerian theory.

25. Here it should be acknowledged that this chapter generally privileges pitch over rhythm. That is, passages of music are often contrasted on the basis of differing pitch complexity, even though they may not be so different rhythmically (or in terms of other parameters).

26. Although it is difficult to tell conclusively from the recording, both of these passages are likely played by alternating three strokes on an open string with three stopped notes on the adjacent lower string.

27. On the recording Reinhardt plays the bass line along with the bassist while accompanying Grappelli's rendition of the melody.

28. Like many of this article's speculations, this claim is clearly not verifiable. Still, like my conjectures that Reinhardt might have sustained a mental image of a theme's melody and harmonic structure while improvising, it is somewhat corroborated by the accounts of other performers. For instance, in a 1992 master class at the University of New Hampshire, Durham, the jazz pianist John Bunch commented that when playing up-tempo, unaccompanied improvisations he would often imagine a drummer accompanying him. This is akin to the "repetitive rhythmic ostinato" of which I hypothesize here, although, of course, a drum accompaniment, unlike a guitar's, lacks pitch (and, unlike Bunch, Reinhardt was playing with an accompaniment).

29. Ed Sarath, "A New Look at Improvisation," *Journal of Music Theory* 40/1 (1996): 1–38.

30. Ibid., 8–12.

31. "External sounds" can include the preceding improvised melody, as well as the contributions of other members of the ensemble, or even, more rarely, sounds originating outside of the ensemble altogether.

32. This statement represents my oversimplification of Sarath's account; it is conceivable that a repetitive passage might well indicate a higher rate of cognitive event cycles should the performer constantly be evading a continuation that would, in context, be a more routine possibility. See Sarath, "A New Look at Improvisation," 11.

33. Quoted in Balliett, *American Musicians II,* 485.

34. Sarath, "A New Look at Improvisation," 8–9.

35. Quoted in Balliett, *American Musicians II,* 485.

CHAPTER 3

1. Albert B. Lord, *The Singer of Tales,* 2nd ed. (Cambridge: Harvard University Press, 2000 [1960]).

2. Ibid., 65, 4.

3. Within two years of the publication of Lord's *The Singer of Tales* in 1960, the media theorist Marshall McLuhan may have been the first to explicitly relate it to the world of jazz improvisation, writing that "a reverse perspective of the literate Western world is the one afforded to the reader of Albert Lord's *Singer of Tales.* But we also live in an electric or post-literate time when the jazz musician uses all the techniques of oral poetry" (Marshall McLuhan, *Essential McLuhan,* ed. Eric McLuhan and Frank Zingrone [New York: Basic Books, 1995], 98, first published in Marshall McLuhan, *The Gutenberg Galaxy: The Making of Typographic Man* [Toronto: University of Toronto Press, 1962]).

4. Thomas Owens, "Charlie Parker: Techniques of Improvisation," PhD diss., 2 volumes, University of California, Los Angeles, 1974. Owens did not reference Parry and Lord's work in his dissertation; the first significant publication to adapt their theory to a musical context was Leo Treitler's "Homer and Gregory: The Transmission of Epic Poetry and Plainchant," *Musical Quarterly* 60/3 (July 1974): 333–72. Also see Treitler's "'Centonate' Chant: *Übles Flickwerk* or *E Pluribus Unus?*" *Journal of the American Musicological Society* 28/1 (1975): 1–23.

5. Lawrence Gushee, "Lester Young's 'Shoe Shine Boy,'" in *Report of the Twelfth Congress, Berkeley, 1977,* International Musicological Society, ed. Daniel Heartz and Bonnie Wade (Kassel: Bärenreiter, 1981); Barry Kernfeld, "Two Coltranes," *Annual Review of Jazz Studies* 2 (1983): 7–66; Gregory Eugene Smith, "Homer, Gregory, and Bill Evans: The Theory of Formulaic Composition in the Context of Jazz Piano Improvisation," PhD diss., Harvard University, 1983.

6. Gushee, "Lester Young's 'Shoe Shine Boy,'" 164.

7. Kernfeld identifies twenty-six formulas in Coltrane's playing and then abstracts four basic "families of recurring cells," each between sixteen and fifty-two notes in length, such that every formula represents a segment of at least one of the four families. This enables him to disclose relationships between elements of Coltrane's formulaic vocabulary that are individually dissimilar but nonetheless belong to the same cell family ("Two Coltranes," 38).

8. Ibid., 17. These issues are discussed in Jonathan Finkelman, "Charlie Christian and the Role of Formulas in Jazz Improvisation," *Jazzforschung* 29 (1997): 160–61. Finkelman also gives a succinct summary of Smith's objections to the work of Owens, Gushee, and Kernfeld.

9. Smith, "Homer, Gregory, and Bill Evans," 181.

10. See, for instance, Smith's melodic patterns nos. 21–27 or 62–66 (ibid., 201, 203).

11. Spring determines that Christian often expanded a basic "core" formula with a number of recurrent melodic prefixes and suffixes (Howard Spring, "The Use of Formulas in the Improvisations of Charlie Christian," *Jazzforschung* 22 [1990]: 11–51).

12. Finkelman, "Charlie Christian and the Role of Formulas in Jazz Improvisation," 163.

13. See, for instance, Kernfeld, "Two Coltranes."

14. The transcriptions can be found in the second volume of my doctoral dissertation, "Django Reinhardt's Style and Improvisational Process," PhD diss., 2 volumes, Yale University, 2003.

15. See Paul Vernon, *Jean "Django" Reinhardt: A Contextual Bio-discography, 1910–1953* (Aldershot: Ashgate, 2003).

16. It should furthermore be acknowledged that these definitions are to an extent self-justifying. A given entity's variability depends on the range of phenomena the observer identifies as instances of that entity. Thus, a formula's stability is a product of the strictness of its definition.

17. In the present sense, superformulas are somewhat akin to what Henry Martin describes as "licks," which he sees as "more elaborately composed or patterned" than "pathways," which tend to be shorter and are analogous to the formulas I call variable. See Martin's *Charlie Parker and Thematic Improvisation,* 116.

18. Owens, "Charlie Parker," 1: 269. Parker's career was approximately a decade shorter than Reinhardt's.

19. It is worth noting that the formulas listed here might not all be unique to Reinhardt's work. Formula 32, for example, is very similar to a device employed by tenor saxophonist Lester Young, which appears during the final eight bars of his famous 1936 solo on Gershwin's "Oh, Lady Be Good!" Transcriptions can be found in Gunther Schuller, *The Swing Era: The Development of Jazz, 1930–1945* (New York: Oxford University Press, 1989), 231–32; Lewis Porter, *Lester Young,* rev. ed. (Ann Arbor: University of Michigan Press, 2005) 90; and Bernard Cash, "Trumbauer, Parker, and Young," in *A Lester Young Reader,* ed. Lewis Porter (Washington, DC: Smithsonian Institution Press, 1991), 273–74. Louis Gottlieb states that this formula disappeared from Young's playing in his later recordings ("Why So Sad, Pres?" in *A Lester Young Reader,* 220–21).

20. Kernfeld, "Two Coltranes."

21. There is a more sophisticated possible interpretation of mm. 12.8–12.9 of "Festival Swing." While the bassist on the recording, Tony Rovira, plays a bass line implying the harmonic progression from C major to G7 notated here, by the 1940s younger musicians of the bebop generation were using new harmonic variations on the standard twelve-bar blues form. One of the most common alternate forms used a circle-of-fifths progression, III–VI in m. 8, II in m. 9, and V7 in m. 10. ♭III could also be used as a tritone substitution for VI on the third and fourth beats of m. 8. Thus, a C-major blues might follow the harmonic progression E minor–E♭ minor (m. 8), D minor (m. 9), and G7 (m. 10). (Often minor-seventh

chords would be used instead of simple triads for each harmony.) Thus, Reinhardt's improvised melody in these measures of "Festival Swing" could be read as implying a harmonic progression of this sort. D and B are the fifth and minor-seventh of E minor, B♭ (the final eighth-note of m. 12.8) is the fifth of E♭ minor, and the F-major arpeggiation in m. 12.9 suggests the third, fifth, and seventh of a D-minor harmony rather than the G7 played by the bass player.

CHAPTER 4

1. Steve Larson, "Dave McKenna's Performance of 'Have You Met Miss Jones?'," *American Music* 11 (1993): 293–94.

2. The classic theory of interaction in jazz improvisation is Ingrid Monson, *Saying Something: Jazz Improvisation and Interaction* (Chicago: University of Chicago Press, 1996).

3. The specific form in which the labeled motives appear varies significantly. For instance, in m. 2.14, the first instance of β, F15 occurs at a lower pitch level than the initial note of F2, while in the other iterations of β it appears at a slightly higher pitch level, altering the general, melodic contour of the combined motive. Still, the two labeled motives each have consistent basic melodic profiles.

4. Leonard B. Meyer, *Style and Music: Theory, History, and Ideology* (Chicago: University of Chicago Press, 1989).

5. Ibid., 44–48. Strict transposition is associated with chromaticism and modulation just as motivic transposition within a given diatonic system generally involves intervallic adjustments.

6. Note that the figure in m. 2.12 that introduces a new four-bar unit is here classified as a structural marker because it resembles other such markers that Reinhardt sometimes played while accompanying others, as can be heard on "Echoes of France" (1/31/46; mx. OEF 28-1) from the same recording session. Also, the figure in m. 2.24 is assigned to the conceptual background mainly because of its soft dynamic level and because it is essentially an embellished "echo" of the preceding B♭–E♭ motive, which invokes the original melody.

7. Note furthermore that the passage occurring between mm. 2.1 and 2.4 recurs under modification in mm. 2.18–2.20 where, at the equivalent point during the second half of this ABAC thirty-two-bar form, it is shifted several beats later than its original location.

8. The figure beginning at the end of m. 3.14 is, for present purposes, classified as an instance of F14 even though, strictly speaking, it does not contain an initial lower-neighbor prefix.

CHAPTER 5

1. A chronological table outlining Reinhardt's stylistic development is provided in Alexander Schmitz and Peter Maier, *Django Reinhardt: Sein Leben, seine Musik, seine Schallplatten* (Buchendorf: Oreos Verlag, 1985), 226–27.

2. Scott DeVeaux, *The Birth of Bebop* (Berkeley: University of California Press, 1997), 92.

3. Ibid., 78.

4. Tritone substitution occurs when a given harmony is replaced by the chord a tritone away, often during a cycle-of-fifths progression so as to create chromatically descending harmonic (and, by extension, melodic) motion. For example, by substituting a ♭II7 harmony for a dominant (V7) harmony, a II–V7–I progression becomes II–♭II7–I.

5. DeVeaux, *The Birth of Bebop,* 92.

6. Charles Delaunay, *Django Reinhardt,* trans. Michael James (New York: Da Capo, 1981 [1961]), 73, 89; John Chilton, *The Song of the Hawk: The Life and Recordings of Coleman Hawkins* (London: Quartet, 1990), 141.

7. Thomas Owens, *Bebop: The Music and Its Players* (New York: Oxford University Press, 1995), 36.

8. For an brief overview of Schenkerian analytic notation, see Henry Martin, *Charlie Parker and Thematic Improvisation* (Lanham, MD: Scarecrow, 1996), 9–39. For a more extensive introduction, see Allen Forte and Steven E. Gilbert, *Introduction to Schenkerian Analysis* (New York: Norton, 1982).

9. Figure 5.1 indicates an unconventional voiceleading motion in the second staff, where the note B♭—the minor seventh of the dominant harmony, C (labeled a neighbor note, N)—resolves upward to C rather than following an orthodox stepwise descent to A, the third scale degree. The proposed reading takes into consideration these pitches' strong metric location (they appear on the downbeats).

10. Leonard B. Meyer, *Style and Music: Theory, History, and Ideology* (Chicago: University of Chicago Press, 1989), 3.

11. Ibid., 137.

12. For instance, the pianist Kenny Barron, who, although he is of a more recent generation than bebop's originators, remains grounded in that style's conventions, notes, "[W]e have a tendency to end phrases or to end lines almost without fail on the first, third, fifth, seventh, or ninth degrees of a chord" (quoted in Berliner, *Thinking in Jazz,* 212).

13. The E-minor harmony indicated in this measure could admittedly be questioned both because the bass is difficult to hear clearly on the recording and because the A sections of "I Got Rhythm" chord progressions appear in many variant forms. With respect to the melodic use of a minor harmony's major third, the bassist Chuck Israels comments, "[T]here are few notes that sound as awful as a major third on a minor chord or that would be any more difficult to resolve" (quoted in ibid., 211).

14. Steven Strunk, "Bebop Melodic Lines: Tonal Characteristics," *Annual Review of Jazz Studies* 3 (1985): 99.

15. Steve Larson, "Schenkerian Analysis of Modern Jazz: Questions about Method," *Music Theory Spectrum* 20/2 [1998]: 215–16.

16. Thomas Owens, "Charlie Parker: Techniques of Improvisation," PhD diss., University of California, Los Angeles, 1974, 2:3.

17. DeVeaux, *The Birth of Bebop*, 261.

18. Although the two pitches heard in m. 3.16, C and G, could be interpreted as the root and fifth of a C(-major) harmony, the pitch G strongly suggests a non-chord tone not only because the original harmony, played by the rhythm section, is F7 but also because in the following measures Reinhardt clearly treats G♮ as an upper neighbor to F (albeit in the context of a B♭ harmony rather than F major).

19. Owens, "Charlie Parker," 2: 1.

20. By December 1953, King Pleasure was inspired to record a vocalese version of "Parker's Mood" (singing lyrics to the saxophone solo), something that was usually done with jazz instrumental recordings that were famous enough to be recognized by many listeners.

21. Owens, "Charlie Parker," 2: 2, 4. For a transcription of Parker's solo, see Carl Woideck, *Charlie Parker: His Music and Life* (Ann Arbor: University of Michigan Press, 1996), 237–39.

22. See the commentary on these passages in Woideck, *Charlie Parker*, 157; and, in the context of a complete analysis, Kwatei Jones-Quartey, "'Parker's Mood' Revisited," *Annual Review of Jazz Studies* 10 (1999): 226.

EPILOGUE

1. For a bibliography of jazz theory publications, see http://music.uncg .edu:2001/ (accessed August 21, 2008).

2. Barry Kernfeld, "Improvisation," in *The New Grove Dictionary of Jazz*, 2nd ed., ed. Barry Kernfeld (New York: Macmillan, 2002), 2:318.

3. Schuller discusses Carter's, Hawkins's, and Eldridge's music in *The Swing Era: The Development of Jazz, 1930–1945* (New York: Oxford University Press, 1989), 373–85, 426–50, 450–63. Scott DeVeaux addresses Hawkins in *The Birth of Bebop* (Berkeley: University of California Press, 1997), 72–115. Although these are valuable contributions, they are all relatively minor components of books whose scope is much broader.

❀ BIBLIOGRAPHY ❀

Ansermet, Ernest. "Sur un Orchestre Nègre." *Revue Romande,* October 1919. Reprinted in *Keeping Time: Readings in Jazz History,* ed. Robert Walser, 9–11. New York: Oxford University Press, 1999.

Antonietto, Alain. "La Main de Django." *Études Tsiganes* 2 (1984): 41–48.

Atkins, Chet, with Bill Neely. *Country Gentleman.* Chicago: Regnery, 1974.

Balliett, Whitney. *American Musicians II: Seventy-two Portraits in Jazz.* New York: Oxford University Press, 1996.

Balliett, Whitney. "Seeing Music." *New Yorker,* September 11, 2000, 98–100.

Balliett, Whitney. *Collected Works: A Journal of Jazz, 1954–2000.* New York: St. Martin's, 2000.

Balmer, Paul. *Stéphane Grappelli: With and without Django.* London: Sanctuary, 2003.

Bechet, Sidney. *Treat It Gentle.* New York: Da Capo, 2002 [1960].

Berliner, Paul F. *Thinking in Jazz: The Infinite Art of Improvisation.* Chicago: University of Chicago Press, 1994.

Billard, François. *Django Reinhardt: Un géant sur son nuage.* Paris: Lieu Commun, 1993.

Blake, Jody. *Le Tumulte noir: Modernist Art and Popular Entertainment in Jazz-Age Paris, 1900–1930.* University Park: Pennsylvania State University Press, 1999.

Blancq, Charles. *Sonny Rollins: The Journey of a Jazzman.* Boston: Twayne, 1983.

Boswick, John A., Jr. "Rehabilitation of the Burned Hand." *Clinical Orthopaedics* 104 (1974): 162–74.

Bregman, Albert. *Auditory Scene Analysis: The Perceptual Organization of Sound.* Cambridge: MIT Press, 1990.

Cash, Bernard. "Trumbauer, Parker, and Young." In *A Lester Young Reader,* ed. Lewis Porter, 264–76. Washington, DC: Smithsonian Institution Press, 1991.

Cherlin, Michael. "Dialectical Opposition in Schoenberg's Music and Thought." *Music Theory Spectrum* 22/2 (2000): 157–76.

Chilton, John. *The Song of the Hawk: The Life and Recordings of Coleman Hawkins.* London: Quartet, 1990.

Cone, Edward T. "Stravinsky: The Progress of a Method." In *Music: A View from Delft: Selected Essays,* ed. Robert P. Morgan, 293–301. Chicago: University of Chicago Press, 1989.

Covach, John. "We Won't Get Fooled Again: Rock Music and Musical Analysis." In *Keeping Score: Music, Interdisciplinarity, and Culture,* ed. David Schwarz, Anahid Kassabian, and Lawrence Siegel, 75–89. Charlottesville: University of Virginia Press, 1997.

Cruickshank, Ian. *The Guitar Style of Django Reinhardt and the Gypsies.* London: Wise, 1989.

Delaunay, Charles. *Django Reinhardt.* Trans. Michael James. London: Cassell, 1961. Reprinted by Da Capo in 1981.

DeVeaux, Scott. *The Birth of Bebop.* Berkeley: University of California Press, 1997.

DeVeaux, Scott. "Constructing the Jazz Tradition." In *The Jazz Cadence of American Culture,* ed. Robert G. O'Meally, 483–512. New York: Columbia University Press, 1998.

Dregni, Michael. *Django: The Life and Music of a Gypsy Legend.* New York: Oxford University Press, 2004.

Dregni, Michael. *Gypsy Jazz: In Search of Django Reinhardt and the Soul of Gypsy Swing.* New York: Oxford University Press, 2008.

Dregni, Michael, with Alain Antonietto and Anne Legrand. *Django Reinhardt and the Illustrated History of Gypsy Jazz.* Denver: Speck, 2006.

"11 Leaders on *Down Beat*'s All-American 1939 Band." *Down Beat,* January 1, 1940, 13.

Ferris, Leonard. "Mary Osborne: A Unique Roll [*sic*] in Jazz Guitar History." In *Jazz Guitarists: Collected Interviews from* Guitar Player *Magazine,* 78–79. Saratoga, CA: Guitar Player Productions, 1975.

"Final Results of Band Contest." *Down Beat,* January 1939: 17.

Finkelman, Jonathan. "Charlie Christian and the Role of Formulas in Jazz Improvisation." *Jazzforschung* 29 (1997): 159–88.

Floyd, Samuel A., Jr. *The Power of Black Music: Interpreting Its History from Africa to the United States.* New York: Oxford University Press, 1995.

Forte, Allen, and Steven E. Gilbert. *Introduction to Schenkerian Analysis.* New York: Norton, 1982.

Galamian, Ivan. *Principles of Violin Playing and Teaching.* Englewood Cliffs, NJ: Prentice-Hall, 1962.

Gennari, John. *Blowin' Hot and Cool: Jazz and Its Critics.* Chicago: University of Chicago Press, 2006.

Giddins, Gary. *Satchmo.* New York: Dolphin, 1988.

Givan, Benjamin. "Jazz Taxonomies." *Jazz Research News* 10 (2003): 476–80.

Givan, Benjamin. "Django Reinhardt's Style and Improvisational Process." PhD diss., 2 volumes, Yale University, 2003.

Givan, Benjamin. "Django Reinhardt's Left Hand." In *Jazz Planet,* ed. E. Taylor Atkins, 19–39. Jackson: University Press of Mississippi, 2003.

Givan, Benjamin. "Duets for One: Louis Armstrong's Vocal Recordings." *Musical Quarterly* 87/2 (2004): 188–218.

Gottlieb, Louis. "Why So Sad, Pres?" In *A Lester Young Reader,* ed. Lewis Porter, 211–23. Washington, DC: Smithsonian Institution Press, 1991.

Grappelli, Stéphane, with Joseph Oldenhove and Jean-Marc Bramy. *Mon Violon pour Tout Bagage: Mémoires.* Paris: Calman-Lvy, 1992.

Green, Jeffrey. "'In Dahomey' in London in 1903." *The Black Perspective in Music* 11/1 (1983): 22–40.

Gushee, Lawrence. "Lester Young's 'Shoe Shine Boy.'" In *Report of the Twelfth Congress, Berkeley, 1977,* International Musicological Society, ed. Daniel Heartz and Bonnie Wade, 151–68. Kassel: Bärenreiter, 1981.

Harker, Brian. "'Telling a Story': Louis Armstrong and Coherence in Early Jazz." *Current Musicology* 63 (1999): 46–83.

Hartman, Charles O. *Jazz Text: Voice and Improvisation in Poetry, Jazz, and Song.* Princeton: Princeton University Press, 1991.

Hobsbawm, Eric, and Terence Ranger, eds. *The Invention of Tradition.* Cambridge: Cambridge University Press, 1983.

Hodeir, André. *Jazz: Its Evolution and Essence.* Trans. David Noakes. New York: Grove, 1956.

Hodeir, André. *Toward Jazz.* Trans. Noel Burch. New York: Grove, 1962.

Hodeir, André. *The André Hodeir Reader,* ed. Jean-Louis Pautrot. Ann Arbor: University of Michigan Press, 2006.

Hoefer, George. "The Magnificent Gypsy." *Down Beat,* July 1966, 21–25, 60–61.

Horricks, Raymond. *Stéphane Grappelli.* Tunbridge Wells: Baton, 1983.

Jackson, Jeffrey H. *Making Jazz French: Music and Modern Life in Interwar Paris.* Durham: Duke University Press, 2003.

Jalard, Michel-Claude. "Django et l'école tsigane du jazz." *Les Cahiers du Jazz* 1 (1959): 54–73.

James, Michael, with Howard Rye and Barry Kernfeld. "Django Reinhardt." In *The New Grove Dictionary of Jazz,* ed. Barry Kernfeld, 3: 396–97. London: Macmillan, 2002.

Jones, LeRoi [Amiri Baraka]. "Jazz and the White Critic." In *Black Music,* 11–20. New York: Da Capo, 1998 [1968].

Jones-Quartey, Kwatei. "'Parker's Mood' Revisited." *Annual Review of Jazz Studies* 10 (1999): 221–35.

Jorgenson, John. "Gypsy Guitar Primer." *Acoustic Guitar,* February 1996, 40–42.

Jorgenson, John. "Django for a Day." *Acoustic Guitar,* July 2004, 34–42.

Jost, Ekkehard. "Jazz, Musette und Cante Flamenco: Traditionslinien in der Musik der französischen Gitans und Manouches." In *Die Musik der Sinti und Roma.* Vol. 2: *Der Sinti-Jazz,* ed. Anita Awosusi, 15–27. Heidelberg: Schriftenreihe des Dokumentations und Kulturzentrums Deutscher Sinti und Roma, 1997.

Kennedy, Rick. *Jelly Roll, Bix, and Hoagy: Gennett Studios and the Birth of Recorded Jazz.* Bloomington: Indiana University Press, 1994.

Kenney, William Howland. "Historical Context and the Definition of Jazz: Putting More of the History in 'Jazz History.'" In *Jazz among the Discourses,* ed. Krin Gabbard, 100–16. Durham: Duke University Press, 1995.

Kernfeld, Barry. "Adderley, Coltrane, and Davis at the Twilight of Bebop: The Search for Melodic Coherence." PhD diss., Cornell University, 1981.

Kernfeld, Barry. "Two Coltranes." *Annual Review of Jazz Studies* 2 (1983): 7–66.

Kernfeld, Barry. *What to Listen for in Jazz*. New Haven: Yale University Press, 1995.

Kienzle, Rich. *Great Guitarists*. New York: Facts on File, 1985.

King, B. B. with David Ritz. *Blues All around Me: The Autobiography of B. B. King*. New York: Avon, 1996.

Koepke, George H., Barbara Feallock, and Irving Feller. "Splinting the Severely Burned Hand." *American Journal of Occupational Therapy* 17 (1963): 147–50.

Kramer, Jonathan. "Moment Form in Twentieth-Century Music." *Musical Quarterly* 64 (1978): 177–94.

Larson, Steve. "Dave McKenna's Performance of 'Have You Met Miss Jones'?" *American Music* 11 (1993): 283–315.

Larson, Steve. "Schenkerian Analysis of Modern Jazz: Questions about Method." *Music Theory Spectrum* 20/2 (1998): 209–41.

Larson, Steve. "Swing and Motive in Three Performances by Oscar Peterson." *Journal of Music Theory* 43/2 (1999): 283–314.

Larson, Steve. "Composition versus Improvisation?" *Journal of Music Theory* 49/2 (2005): 241–73.

Lee, Bill. "Barney Kessel." In *Jazz Guitarists: Collected Interviews from* Guitar Player *Magazine,* 56–59. Saratoga, CA: Guitar Player Productions, 1975.

Lord, Albert. *The Singer of Tales*. 2nd ed. Cambridge: Harvard University Press, 2000 [1960].

Martin, Henry. *Charlie Parker and Thematic Improvisation*. Lanham, MD: Scarecrow, 1996.

Martin, Henry. "Jazz Theory: An Overview." *Annual Review of Jazz Studies* 8 (1996): 1–17.

McLuhan, Marshall. *The Gutenberg Galaxy: The Making of Typographic Man*. Toronto: University of Toronto Press, 1962.

McLuhan, Marshall. *Essential McLuhan*. Ed. Eric McLuhan and Frank Zingrone. New York: Basic Books, 1995.

Menn, Don, ed. *Secrets from the Masters: Conversations with Forty Great Guitar Players*. San Francisco: Miller Freeman, 1992.

Meyer, Leonard B. *Style and Music: Theory, History, and Ideology*. Chicago: University of Chicago Press, 1989.

Monson, Ingrid. *Saying Something: Jazz Improvisation and Interaction*. Chicago: University of Chicago Press, 1996.

Murray, Albert. *Stomping the Blues*. New York: McGraw-Hill, 1976.

Nabe, Marc-Edouard. *Nuage*. Paris: Le Dilettante, 1993.

Neill, Billy, and E. Gates. *Discography of the Recorded Works of Django Reinhardt and the Quintette du Hot Club de France*. London: Clifford Essex Music, 1944.

Nichols, H. Minor. *Manual of Hand Injuries*. Chicago: Year Book, 1955.

Nichols, Roger. *The Harlequin Years: Music in Paris, 1917–1929*. Berkeley: University of California Press, 2002.

Obrecht, Jas, ed. *Rollin' and Tumblin': The Postwar Blues Guitarists*. San Francisco: Miller Freeman, 2000.

Odell, Jay Scott, and Robert B. Winans. "Banjo." In *The New Grove Dictionary of Music and Musicians,* ed. Stanley Sadie, 2:660–65. London: Macmillan, 2001.

Owens, Thomas. "Charlie Parker: Techniques of Improvisation." PhD diss., 2 volumes, University of California, Los Angeles, 1974.

Owens, Thomas. *Bebop: The Music and Its Players.* New York: Oxford University Press, 1995.

Owens, Thomas. "Analysing Jazz." In *The Cambridge Companion to Jazz,* ed. Mervyn Cooke and David Horn, 286–97. Cambridge: Cambridge University Press, 2002.

Peters, Mike. "Teach-In: Django Reinhardt." *Sing Out!* 29/1 (1982): 12–15.

Peters, Mike. Liner notes to *The Complete Django Reinhardt and Quintet of the Hot Club of France Swing/HMV Sessions, 1936–1948.* Mosaic MD6-190, 1999.

Porter, Lewis. *Lester Young.* Rev. ed. Ann Arbor: University of Michigan Press, 2005.

Ratliff, Ben. "A Delirium of Gypsy Music Barrels Along in Overdrive." *New York Times,* December 4, 2000, E5.

Rasula, Jed. "The Media of Memory: The Seductive Menace of Records in Jazz History." In *Jazz among the Discourses,* ed. Krin Gabbard, 134–62. Durham: Duke University Press, 1995.

Rosen, Steve. "Mahavishnu John McLaughlin." In *Jazz Guitarists: Collected Interviews from* Guitar Player *Magazine,* 72–74. Saratoga, CA: Guitar Player Productions, 1975.

Sarath, Ed. "A New Look at Improvisation." *Journal of Music Theory* 40/1 (1996): 1–38.

Schmitz, Alexander. "Stilprägende Elemente in der Musik von Django Reinhardt." In *Die Musik der Sinti und Roma.* Vol. 2: *Der Sinti-Jazz,* ed. Anita Awosusi, 29–45. Heidelberg: Schriftenreihe des Dokumentations und Kulturzentrums Deutscher Sinti und Roma, 1997.

Schmitz, Alexander, and Peter Maier. *Django Reinhardt: sein Leben, seine Musik, seine Schallplatten.* Buchendorf: Oreos Verlag, 1985.

Schuller, Gunther. "Sonny Rollins and the Challenge of Thematic Improvisation." *Jazz Review* 1/1 (November 1958): 6–11, 21. Reprinted in Gunther Schuller, *Musings: The Musical Worlds of Gunther Schuller,* 86–97. New York: Oxford University Press, 1986.

Schuller, Gunther. *The Swing Era: The Development of Jazz, 1930–1945.* New York: Oxford University Press, 1989.

Shack, William A. *Harlem in Montmartre: A Paris Jazz Story between the Great Wars.* Berkeley: University of California Press, 2001.

Shaughnessy, Mary Alice. *Les Paul: An American Original.* New York: Morrow, 1993.

Smith, Geoffrey. *Stéphane Grappelli.* London: Pavilion, 1997.

Smith, Gregory Eugene. "Homer, Gregory, and Bill Evans: The Theory of Formulaic Composition in the Context of Jazz Piano Improvisation." PhD diss., Harvard University, 1983.

Spring, Howard. "The Use of Formulas in the Improvisations of Charlie Christian." *Jazzforschung* 22 (1990): 11–51.

Stewart, Rex. *Boy Meets Horn.* Ed. Claire P. Gordon. Ann Arbor: University of Michigan Press, 1991.

Stovall, Tyler. *Paris Noir: African Americans in the City of Light.* Boston: Mariner, 1996.

Strunk, Steven. "Bebop Melodic Lines: Tonal Characteristics." *Annual Review of Jazz Studies* 3 (1985): 97–120.

Sudhalter, Richard M. *Lost Chords: White Musicians and Their Contribution to Jazz, 1915–1945.* New York: Oxford University Press, 1999.

Sullivan, Jack. *New World Symphonies: How American Culture Changed European Music.* New Haven: Yale University Press, 1999.

Taruskin, Richard. *The Oxford History of Western Music.* New York: Oxford University Press, 2005.

Tenzer, Michael. "Introduction: Analysis, Categorization, and Theory of Musics of the World." In *Analytical Studies in World Music,* ed. Michael Tenzer, 3–38. New York: Oxford University Press, 2006.

Tomlinson, Gary. "Cultural Dialogics and Jazz: A White Historian Signifies." In *Disciplining Music,* ed. Katherine Bergeron and Philip V. Bohlman, 64–94. Chicago: University of Chicago Press, 1992.

Treitler, Leo. "Homer and Gregory: The Transmission of Epic Poetry and Plainchant." *Musical Quarterly* 60 (1974): 333–72.

Treitler, Leo. "Centonate Chant: *Übles Flickwerk* or *E Pluribus Unus?*" *Journal of the American Musicological Society* 28 (1975): 1–23.

Tubiana, Raoul. "Movements of the Fingers." *Medical Problems of Performing Artists* 3/4 (1998): 123–28.

Tubiana, Raoul. "Anatomy of the Hand and Upper Limb." In *Medical Problems of the Instrumentalist Musician,* ed. Raoul Tubiana and Peter C. Amadio, 5–53. London: Dunitz, 2000.

Tubiana, Raoul, and Philippe Chamagne. "Functional Anatomy of the Hand." *Medical Problems of Performing Artists* 3/3 (1988): 83–87.

van der Bliek, Rob. "Wes Montgomery: A Study of Coherence in Jazz Improvisation." *Jazzforschung* 23 (1991): 117–78.

Vernon, Paul. *Jean "Django" Reinhardt: A Contextual Bio-discography, 1910–1953.* Aldershot: Ashgate, 2003.

Walser, Robert. "'Out of Notes': Signification, Interpretation, and the Problem of Miles Davis." In *Jazz among the Discourses,* ed. Krin Gabbard, 165–88. Durham: Duke University Press, 1995.

Walser, Robert. "Deep Jazz: Notes on Race, Interiority, and Criticism." In *Inventing the Psychological: Toward a Cultural History of Emotional Life in America,* ed. Joel Pfister and Nancy Schnog, 271–96. New Haven: Yale University Press, 1997.

Ward, Geoffrey C., and Ken Burns. *Jazz: A History of America's Music.* New York: Knopf, 2000.

Williams, J. Kent. "Authors' Responses to Forte's Questions." *Annual Review of Jazz Studies* 9 (1997–98): 104–5.

Williams, Patrick. *Django Reinhardt.* Marseilles: Éditions Parenthèses, 1998.

Williams, Patrick. *Gypsy World: The Silence of the Living and the Voices of the Dead.* Trans. Catherine Tihanyi. Chicago: University of Chicago Press, 2003.

Woideck, Carl. *Charlie Parker: His Music and Life.* Ann Arbor: University of Michigan Press, 1996.

Zwerin, Mike. "Jazz in Europe." In *The Oxford Companion to Jazz,* ed. Bill Kirchner, 534–47. New York: Oxford University Press, 2000.

◉ DISCOGRAPHY ◉

For a comprehensive discography with full personnel listings, readers should consult Paul Vernon's *Jean "Django" Reinhardt: A Contextual Bio-Discography 1910–1953*. Reinhardt's recordings have entered the public domain in Europe and are continually reissued on different compact disc (CD) compilations, most of which go rapidly out of print. Almost all of the original tracks are readily available in one form or another as of this writing.

The following discography consists of (1) a list of some recent CD compilations with boldface abbreviations; (2) a list of all the Reinhardt recordings mentioned in this book, along with their dates and matrix numbers, keyed by means of boldface abbreviations to one of the CD compilations on which each track has been reissued; (3) a single film entry; and (4) a list of other musicians' recordings that this book has referenced.

COMPACT DISC REISSUES: ABBREVIATIONS

CDR *The Complete Django Reinhardt and Quintet of the Hot Club of France Swing/HMV Sessions, 1936–1948.* Mosaic MD6-190.

CER *The Classic Early Recordings in Chronological Order.* JSP JSPCD 901.

BP *Django Reinhardt and the Hot Club of France Quintet: Brussels 1947, Paris 1951, 1952, 1953.* DRG 8473.

D49 *Djangology '49.* Bluebird 9988-2-RB.

DAF *Django with His American Friends.* DRG 8493.

DRB *Django Reinhardt, Vol. 4: En Belgique.* Jazz Archives 157 972.

FR *Django Reinhardt, Quintet of the Hot Club of France: First Recordings!* Prestige OJCCD-1895-2 (P-7614).

IDR1 *Intégrale Django Reinhardt 1: "Presentation Stomp"—The Complete Django Reinhardt (1928–1934).* Frémaux et Associés FA 301.

PM *Peche à la Mouche: The Great Blue Star Sessions, 1947, 1953.* Verve 835 418-2.

PS *Parisian Swing: Django Reinhardt and Stéphane Grappelli with the Quintet of the Hot Club of France.* Avid AMSC 648.

S *Souvenirs: Django Reinhardt and Stéphane Grappelli with the Quintet of the Hot Club of France.* London/Decca 820 591-2.

"After You've Gone" (1–2/49; mx. CW 49). **D49**
"Ain't Misbehavin'" (4/22/37; mx. OLA 1708-1). **CDR**
"All the Things You Are" (1-2/49; mx. CW 30). **D49**
"Anniversary Song" (7/6/47; mx. ST 2091-1). **PM**
"Appel Indirect" (6/14/38; mx. 4213-HPP). **PS**
"Avalon" (7/35; mx. P77434). **FR**
"Babik (Bi-Bop)" (take 1) (5/21/47; mx. Fo 1785-R). **BP**
"Babik (Bi-Bop)" (take 2) (5/21/47; mx. Fo 1785-RC). **BP**
"Beyond the Sea" (1–2/49; mx. CW 35). **D49**
"Big Boy Blues" (11/19/37; mx. OLA 1981-1). **DAF**
"Blue Light Blues" (3/7/38; mx. OSW 6-1). **DAF**
"Blue Lou" (3/26/47; mx. OSW 328-1). **PS**
"Blues Clair" (2/26/43; mx. OSW 328-1). **CDR**
"Blues for Ike" (3/10/53; mx. 17276). **PM**
"Body and Soul" (5/31/38; mx. CL 6716-1). **CDR**
"Brazil" (7/18/47; mx. ST 2105). **PM**
"Bricktop" (3/10/48; mx. OSW 504-1). **CDR**
"Bricktop" (1-2/49; mx. CW 56). **D49**
"Bugle Call Rag" (7/7/37; mx. OLA 1884-1). **DAF**
"Charleston" (4/21/37; mx. OLA 1703-1). **CDR**
"Chez Moi à Six Heures" (5/8/42; mx. 16225). **DRB**
"Chicago" (4/26/37; mx. OLA 1713-1). **CDR**
"Confessin' (That I Love You)" (3/35; mx. P 77242). **FR**
"Confessin' (That I Love You)" (3/10/53; mx. 17283). **PM**
"Coquette" (1/31/46; mx. OEF 25-1). **CDR**
"Daphne" (9/29/37; mx. OLA 2149-1). **DAF**
"Daphne" (1/31/38; mx. DTB 3528). **S**
"Daphne" (1–2/49; mx. CW 34). **D49**
"Dinah" (12/34; mx. P 77161). **FR**
"Distraction" (4/16/42; mx. 16190). **DRB**
"Django's Tiger" (1/31/46; mx. OEF 26-1). **CDR**
"Dynamisme" (5/8/42; mx. 16223). **DRB**
"Echoes of France" (1/31/46; mx. OEF 28-1). **CDR**
"Embraceable You (1/31/46; mx. OEF 27-1). **CDR**
"Exactly Like You" (4/21/37; mx. OLA 1702-1). **CDR**
"Festival Swing" (12/26/40; mx. OSW 173-1). **CDR**
"Hallelujah" (1–2/49; mx. CW 24). **D49**
"Hangin' Around Boudon" (7/7/37; mx. OLA 1888-1). **DAF**
"H.C.Q. Strut" (8/25/39; mx. DR 3862-1). **PS**
"Honeysuckle Rose" (1/31/38; mx. DTB 3523-1). **S**
"Honeysuckle Rose" (1–2/49; mx. CW 29). **D49**
"Hot Lips" (4/22/37; mx. OLA 1707-1). **CDR**
"How High the Moon" (3/26/47; mx. OSW 450-1). **CDR**

"Hungaria" (take 1) (3/21/39; mx. 4967-HPP). **PS**

"I Can't Give You Anything But Love" (5/4/36; mx. OLA 1058-1). **CDR**

"I Got Rhythm" (1–2/49; mx. CW 51). **D49**

"I Saw Stars" (1–2/49; mx. CW 52). **D49**

"I Wonder Where My Baby Is Tonight" (5/17/39; mx. 5083-HPP). **PS**

"I'll See You in My Dreams" (6/30/39; mx. OPG 1721-1). **CDR**

"I'm Coming Virginia" (3/7/38; mx. OSW 4-1). **DAF**

"I'se a Muggin'" (5/4/36; mx. OLA 1057-1). **CDR**

"I've Got My Love to Keep Me Warm" (9/1/38; mx. DR 2903-1). **PS**

"I've Had My Moments" (9/35; mx. P 77538). **FR**

"If I Had You" (2/1/38; mx. DTB 3532-1). **PS**

"Impromptu" (5/11/51; mx. P853). **BP**

"In a Sentimental Mood" (4/26/37; mx. OLA 1718-1). **CDR**

"It Had to Be You" (2/1/38; mx. DTB 3533-1). **PS**

"Japanese Sandman" (7/7/37; mx. OLA 1889-1). **DAF**

"Japanese Sandman" (5/17/39; mx. 5081-HPP). **PS**

"Jeepers Creepers" (alternate take) (3/21/39; mx. 4968-1/2HPP). **CER**

"Jeepers Creepers" (master take) (3/21/39; mx. 4968-HPP). **PS**

"Just One of Those Things" (5/21/47; mx. Fo 1787-RC). **BP**

"Lady Be Good" (12/4/34; mx. P77163). **FR**

"Lady Be Good" (9/29/37; mx. OLA 2147-1). **DAF**

"Lady Be Good" (3/10/48; mx. OSW 501-1). **CDR**

"Limehouse Blues" (5/4/36; mx. OLA 1062-1). **CDR**

"A Little Love, A Little Kiss" (4/26/37; mx. OLA 1716-1). **CDR**

"Liza" (2/1/46; mx. DR 10029-1). **S**

"Love's Melody" (2/1/46; mx. DR 10026-1). **S**

"Lover Man" (1–2/49; mx. CW 37). **D49**

"Mabel" (12/14/37; mx. OLA 1997-2). **CDR**

"The Man I Love" (8/25/39; mx. DR 3864-1). **S**

"Marie" (1–2/49; mx. CW 38). **D49**

"Mike" (3/10/48; mx. OSW 500-1). **CDR**

"Minor Blues" (4/16/47; mx. ST 1984). **PM**

"Minor Swing" (11/25/37; mx. OLA 1990-1). **CDR**

"Minor Swing" (1–2/49; mx. CW 40). **D49**

"Miss Annabelle Lee" (4/26/37; mx. OLA 1715-1). **CDR**

"Miss Columbia" (9–10/28; mx. H 966-B). **IDR1**

"Mixture" (4/16/42; mx. 16196). **DRB**

"Moi Aussi" (9–10/28; mx. 968-A). **IDR1**

"Montmartre" (4/5/39; mx. OSW 63-1). **DAF**

"Moonglow" (10/21/35; mx. 2082-HPP). **PS**

"My Melancholy Baby" (3/22/39; mx. 4973-HPP). **PS**

"My Sweet" (1/31/38; mx. DTB 3526-2). **S**

"Nagasaki" (10/15/36; mx. OLA 1290-1). **CDR**

"Ol' Man River" (11/14/47; mx. OSW 483-1). **CDR**

"Paramount Stomp" (12/7/37; mx. OLA 1995-1). **CDR**
"Please Be Kind" (9/1/38; mx. DR 2904-1). **S**
"Porto Cabello" (5/21/47; mx. Fo 1872-RB). **BP**
"R-Vingt Six" (3/26/47; mx. OSW 449-1). **PS**
"Rose Room" (4/22/37; mx. OLA 1709-1). **CDR**
"Runnin' Wild" (4/26/37; mx. OLA 1712-1). **CDR**
"Saint Louis Blues" (9/9/37; mx. OLA 1952-1). **CDR**
"The Sheik of Araby" (4/27/37; mx. OLA 1737-1). **CDR**
"Solid Old Man" (4/5/39; mx. OSW 67-1). **DAF**
"Solitude" (4/21/37; mx. OLA 1706-1). **CDR**
"Songe d'Automne" (5/21/47; mx. Fo 1784-RC). **BP**
"Stompin' at Decca" (1/31/38; mx. DTB 3530-1). **PS**
"Studio 24" (4/16/42; mx. 16192). **DRB**
"The Sunshine of Your Smile" (4/35; mx. P 77353). **FR**
"Sweet Chorus" (10/15/36; mx. OLA 1295-1). **CDR**
"Sweet Georgia Brown" (12/21/37; mx. OLA 2220-1). **CDR**
"Sweet Georgia Brown" (1/31/38; mx. DTB 3524). **S**
"Swing '39" (3/21/39; mx. 4969-1/2HPP). **PS**
"Them There Eyes" (6/14/38; mx. 4211-HPP). **PS**
"Three Little Words" (6/14/38; mx. 4212-HPP). **PS**
"Tiger Rag" (12/34; mx. P 77162). **FR**
"Tornerai" (2/1/38; mx. DTB 3531-1). **PS**

FILM

Stéphane Grappelli: A Life in the Jazz Century. Music on Earth 001. 2002.

RECORDINGS BY OTHER MUSICIANS

Lagréne, Bireli. *Gypsy Project.* Dreyfus 26626. 2001.
Lagréne, Bireli. *Gipsy Project and Friends.* Dreyfus 36638. 2002.
Lagréne, Bireli. *Move.* Dreyfus 36668. 2005.
Lagréne, Bireli. *Djangology/To Bi or Not to Bi.* Dreyfus 36695. 2007.
Lang, Eddie. "A Little Love, A Little Kiss" (5/28/27; mx. W 80941-D).
Parker, Charlie [Tiny Grimes Quintette]. "Red Cross" (9/15/44; mx. S-5713).
Parker, Charlie [Dizzy Gillespie All Star Quintet]. "Shaw 'Nuff" (5/11/45; mx. 566).
Parker, Charlie. "Now's the Time" (11/26/45; mx. S5841).
Parker, Charlie. "Ko Ko" (11/26/45; mx. 5853).
Parker, Charlie. "Parker's Mood" (9/18/48; mx. B903).

Brick Top
By Django Reinhardt and Stephane Grappelly
Copyright © 1937 (Renewed) by Publications Francis Day S.A.
All Rights in the U.S.A. and Canada Controlled by Jewel Music Publishing
    Co., Inc. (ASCAP)
International Copyright Secured. All Rights Reserved.
Used by Permission.

CHARLESTON
Words and Music by CECIL MACK and JIMMY JOHNSON
© 1923 (Renewed) WB MUSIC CORP
All Rights Reserved. Used by Permission of ALFRED PUBLISHING CO.,
    INC.

Charleston
Words and Music by James Johnson and Cecil Mack
FOR EUROPE (EXCL. COMMONWEALTH OF NATIONS, EIRE, GER-
    MANY AUSTRIA, SWITZERLAND AND SPAIN)
© 1923 WB Music Corp, USA
Warner/Chappell North America Ltd, London W6 8BS
FOR COMMONWEALTH OF NATIONS, EIRE, GERMANY AUSTRIA,
    SWITZERLAND AND SPAIN
© 1923 Harms Inc, USA
(50%) Warner/Chappell North America Ltd, London W6 8BS
(50%) Redwood Music Ltd, London NW1 8BD
Reproduced by permission of Faber Music Ltd
All Rights Reserved.

COQUETTE
Words by GUS KAHN, CARMEN LOMBARDO, AND JOHN
    GREEN
© 1928 GILBERT KEYS MUSIC COMPANY & EMI FEIST CATALOG
    INC.
All Rights on behalf of Gilbert Keyes Music Company Administered in the
    U.S. by WB MUSIC CORP.
All Rights Reserved. Used by Permission of ALFRED PUBLISHING CO.,
    INC.

Django's Tiger
By Django Reinhardt and Stephane Grappelly
Copyright © 1963 (Renewed) by Publications Francis Day S.A.
All Rights in the U.S.A. and Canada Controlled by Jewel Music Publishing
    Co., Inc. (ASCAP)
International Copyright Secured. All Rights Reserved.
Used by Permission.

IF I HAD YOU
Words and Music by TED SHAPIRO, JIMMY CAMPBELL and REG CON-
    NELLY
© 1928 (Renewed) CAMPBELL, CONNELLY & CO., LTD.
All Rights for the U.S. and Canada Administered by EMI ROBBINS CATA-
    LOG INC. (Publishing)
and ALFRED PUBLISHING CO., INC. (Print)
All Rights Reserved. Used by Permission of ALFRED PUBLISHING CO.,
    INC.

IF I HAD YOU
Words and Music by Ted Shapiro, Jimmy Campbell and Reg Connelly
© 1928 Campbell Connelly & Co. Limited
All Rights Reserved. International Copyright Secured.
Reprinted by Permission.

IT HAD TO BE YOU
Words by GUS KAHN Music by ISHAM JONES
© 1924 (Renewed) WARNER BROS. INC.
Rights for the Extended Term in the U.S. controlled by GILBERT KEYES
    MUSIC and THE BANTAM MUSIC PUBLISHING CO.
All Rights Administered by WB MUSIC CORP
All Rights Reserved. Used by Permission of ALFRED PUBLISHING CO.,
    INC.

It Had To Be You
Words by Gus Kahn
Music by Isham Jones
© 1924 Remick Music Corp
EMI Music Publishing Ltd
Reproduced by permission of International Music Publications Ltd (a trading
    name of Faber Music Ltd)
All Rights Reserved.

JEEPERS CREEPERS
Words by JOHNNY MERCER Music by HARRY WARREN
© 1938 (Renewed) WB MUSIC CORP
All Rights Reserved. Used by Permission of ALFRED PUBLISHING CO.,
    INC.

LIZA (ALL THE CLOUDS'LL ROLL AWAY)
Words by IRA GERSHWIN and GUS KAHN Music by GEORGE GERSH-
    WIN
© 1929 (Renewed) WB MUSIC CORP.

All Rights in the U.S.A. and Canada Controlled by Jewel Music Publishing
  Co., Inc. (ASCAP)
International Copyright Secured. All Rights Reserved.
Used by Permission.

Montmartre
By Rex Stewart
© 1939 Onyx Publishers
Used by Permission of Concord Music Co.

Nagasaki
Lyric by Mort Dixon
Music by Harry Warren
Copyright © 1928 (Renewed 1956)
Rights for the extended term administered by Fred Ahlert Music Group/Administered by Bug Music
Rights for the extended term administered by Four Jays Music on behalf of
  Harry Warren
All rights to extended renewal term on behalf of Harry Warren (music) owned
  by Four Jays Music
International Copyright Secured All Rights Reserved
Used by Permission

OH, LADY BE GOOD!
Music and Lyrics by GEORGE GERSHWIN and IRA GERSHWIN
© 1924 (Renewed) WB MUSIC CORP
All Rights Reserved. Used by Permission of ALFRED PUBLISHING CO.,
  INC.

Paramount Stomp
By Django Reinhardt and Stephane Grappelly
Copyright © 1942 (Renewed) by Publications Francis Day S.A.
All Rights in the U.S.A. and Canada Controlled by Jewel Music Publishing
  Co., Inc. (ASCAP)
International Copyright Secured. All Rights Reserved.
Used by Permission.

Solid Old Man ("Solid Rock")
By Rex Stewart
© 1939 Onyx Publishers
Used by Permission of Concord Music Co.

SOLITUDE
By DUKE ELLINGTON, EDDIE DE LANGE and IRVING MILLS

Swing '39
By Django Reinhardt and Stephane Grappelly

◉ INDEX ◉

Farmer, Art, 204n7
Ferré, Boulou, 5
Ferret, Jean "Matelot," 5
Ferret, Pierre "Baro," 123
"Festival Swing," 113, 114 ex. 3.4,
  208n21
  formulas in, 84 fig. 3.1, 93
Finkelman, Jonathan, 76, 78, 207n8
formulas, 75, 77
  used by Charlie Christian, 76,
    208n11
  used by John Coltrane, 76, 207n6
  used by Bill Evans, 76
  used by Charlie Parker, 75, 160,
    179, 190, 194–96, 208n17
  used by Reinhardt, 49, 73–74
    in "After You've Gone," 99,
      100–102 ex. 3.1
    in "Blues for Ike," 190, 194
    in "Bricktop," 171, 172 ex. 5.5
    categories of formula, 77–78
    context-specific formulas, 89–90
      fig. 3.1, 97–98
    in "Coquette," 115, 116–18 ex.
      3.5
    in "Django's Tiger," 99, 102,
      103–8 ex. 3.2, 109
    in "Embraceable You," 147,
      148–55 ex. 4.3, 156 fig. 4.5,
      157
    in "Festival Swing," 113, 114 ex.
      3.4
    in "Honeysuckle Rose," 183,
      184–86 ex. 5.19
    in "I'll See You in My Dreams,"
      124–35 ex. 4.1, 135–36,
      138–39 fig. 4.3
    in "Love's Melody, 141, 142–43
      ex. 4.2, 144, 145 fig. 4.4, 146
    in "Mike," 180
    in "Montmartre," 118–19,
      120–21 ex. 3.6
    in "Solitude," 109, 110–12 ex. 3.3
    stable formulas, 85–87 fig. 3.1,
      94–96

superformulas, 88–89 fig. 3.1,
  96–97, 208n17
  in "Sweet Georgia Brown,"
    21–22
  in "Swing '39," 164, 166 ex. 5.2
  variable formulas, 79, 80–85 fig.
    3.1, 90–94
  used by Lester Young, 76, 208n19
  used in nonmusical contexts, 75
Forte, Allen, 206n21, 210n8
Fullbright, Dick, 43

Gates, E., 10, 22, 201n19
Gennari, John, 197n2
Gennett Studios, 202n29
Gershwin, George, as composer. See
  individual song titles
Gilbert, Steven, 210n8
Gillespie, Dizzy (John)
  as composer, 170–71, 177, 181
  influence on Reinhardt, 6, 170–
    71
  trumpet playing of, 159
Goodman, Benny, 203n39
Gordon, Dexter, 190
Grappelli, Stéphane
  career after World War II, 5, 122,
    157
  as composer (see individual song ti-
    tles)
  first meeting with Reinhardt, 3
  letter from Reinhardt, 197n1
  as pianist, 21, 30, 32
  recollections of Reinhardt, 8, 11
  as violinist, 12–13, 15–16 ex. 1.2, 28,
    30, 105–8 ex. 3.2, 162–64 ex.
    5.1
Green, Freddie, 203n39
Grégor (Krikor Kelekian), 3
Gushee, Lawrence
  on André Hodeir, 28
  on Lester Young, 76, 78
gypsy jazz, 5–6, 22, 95, 109

"Hallelujah," 179, 180 ex. 5.12

hand
  anatomy, 9
  injuries, 9–10
  See also "Reinhardt, Django"
Handy, W. C., as composer (*see* individual song titles)
"Hangin' Around Boudon," 82 fig. 3.1, 91
Hartman, Charles, 29
Hawkins, Coleman
  performances with Reinhardt, 160
  saxophone playing of, 159–60, 196, 211n3
"H.C.Q. Strut," 52, 53 ex. 2.14
  formulas in, 80 fig. 3.1
Heller, Benny, 203n39
Henderson, Fletcher, 1
Hillyer, Lonnie, 29, 39
Hindemith, Paul, 3
Hines, Earl, 29
Hodeir, André
  analytical formalism of, 4, 25, 197n1, 204n1
  conception of jazz, 4, 28, 198n15
  Jazz: Its Evolution and Essence (book), 28, 198n15
  on musical discontinuity, 27, 29, 41, 43
  on "Solid Old Man," 26–27, 41, 95
  Toward Jazz (book), 26–27
  as violinist, 4
Hodges, Johnny, 196
Hoefer, George, 201n19
Homer, 75
"Honeysuckle Rose"
  1938 recording of, 30, 34, 183, 184–86 ex. 5.19
  formulas in, 81–82 fig. 3.1, 84 fig. 3.1
  1949 recording of, 183, 186, 187–88 ex. 5.20, 189
Hôpital Lariboisière, 7
Hot Club of France, 3–4
"Hot Lips," 83 fig. 3.1, 90 fig. 3.1
"How High the Moon," 34

formulas in, 81–82 fig. 3.1
"Hungaria," 88 fig. 3.1
hypermetrical downbeat, 39–40, 49, 136, 138, 189

"I Can't Give You Anything But Love," 34, 36–37 ex. 2.5, 39, 54
"If I Had You," 32–34 ex. 2.3, 54
"I Got Rhythm," 177, 210n13
  contrafact themes, 170, 177
  formulas in, 82 fig. 3.1
  tritone substitution in, 181, 182 ex. 5.17
"I'll See You in My Dreams," 124–35 ex. 4.1, 141, 144, 155
  formulas in, 138–39, 139 fig. 4.3
  hypermetrical downbeat, 138 fig. 4.2
  motivic development, 140
  paraphrases in, 136–37, 137 fig. 4.1, 139 fig. 4.3, 147
  thematic exposition, 123, 135
"I'm Coming Virginia," 80 fig. 3.1
"I'm Confessin' That I Love You." *See* "Confessin'"
"Impromptu," 170–71
"In a Sentimental Mood," 30
In Dahomey, 2
interaction (in jazz improvisation), 29–30, 39–40, 45, 139–40, 209n2
"I Saw Stars," 181 ex. 5.15
"I'se a Muggin,'" 80 fig. 3.1
Israels, Chuck, 210n13
"It Had To Be You," 13–14, 15–16 ex. 1.2
  formulas in, 90 fig. 3.1
"I've Got My Love to Keep Me Warm," 30
"I've Had My Moments,' 43, 45–48 ex. 2.11
  formulas in, 86 fig. 3.1
"I Wonder Where My Baby is Tonight," 84 fig. 3.1

Jackson, Jeffrey, 3, 198n6, 198nn12–14